KT-403-224

Pocket Guide to Economics for the Global Investor

John Calverley

AMERICAN
EXPRESS
BANK

Probus Publishing Company

London, England
Burr Ridge, Illinois

First Edition

This edition published in 1995 by

Probus Publishing Company
11 Millers Yard, Mill Lane, Cambridge CB2 1RQ

© 1995 American Express Bank

ALL RIGHTS RESERVED. No part of this publication may be
reproduced, stored in a retrieval system, or transmitted in any
form or by any means, electronic, photocopying, recording or
otherwise, without the prior written permission of the publisher
and the copyright holder.

This publication is designed to provide accurate and
authoritative information in regard to the subject matter
covered. It is sold with the understanding that the publisher is
not engaged in rendering legal, accounting or any other
professional service.

Designed, illustrated and typeset by American Express Bank,
and Elitian Ltd.

ISBN 1 55738 924 1

Printed in the United Kingdom

Contents

Preface

This book is a practical guide to economics for the global investor. It aims to explain the relationships between economic developments, government policies and the markets in a brief, easily digestible form. It is written for all those involved, or just interested, in world markets and investments.

The origin of the book was an idea for a glossary of economics terms to help readers of economics and investment publications. As well as the list of terms it seemed useful to provide a series of clear, simple essays explaining the key aspects of policy and the markets. These essays were distributed during 1994-5 to clients of American Express Bank around the world and proved highly popular. In bringing them together I have added the glossary and an introduction and updated them where necessary.

I would like to thank American Express Bank and especially Richard O'Brien, my predecessor as Chief Economist, for supporting this project. My thanks also to Sarah Brenton who typed and prepared the individual chapters and this collected book. Finally, my thanks to all my colleagues at American Express, especially Sarah Hewin and Tapan Datta, who provided comments and suggestions.

Introduction

"Forecasting is difficult, particularly when it concerns the future".

Economics can feed into investment decisions in two distinct ways. One is to use forecasts of turning points in the business cycle to guide investment decisions. This is often called market timing or tactical asset allocation. The second approach is to use broad forecasts of economic trends or even "themes" to guide investments, often with a longer term horizon. The first approach is used cautiously by most professionals and deserves a "health warning". The second probably brings better rewards over the long term. Either way, theory and experience suggest that the best investment strategy is to diversify widely among different asset classes, e.g. stocks and bonds, and among countries.

Investing over the business cycle

Market timing aims to change the weighting of stocks, bonds and cash according to expectations of the cycle. During a recession bonds are favoured, in the early stage of recovery stocks are highly weighted and towards the peak of the cycle "Cash is King". When practised across countries the aim is to "surf" across markets, picking those with the best prospects, given their individual cycles and relative valuations.

Much of the writing in newspapers and investment publications focuses on the business cycle, for example trying to divine if the economy is showing signs of recovery, or slowing enough, or risking going into recession. The problem is that for these forecasts to be useful, they not only have to be right but they also have to be ahead of everybody else in the market, in practice a tall order!

Forecasting the cycle is difficult in itself. The data we have are always a few months behind and are frequently revised. Lags between policy actions, for example a rise in interest rates and a slow down in the economy, vary. Moreover each business cycle, though similar is also different, with new structural aspects. For example the 1980's upswing was very much influenced by financial liberalisation in many countries while the following downturn was exacerbated by the resulting overhang of debt.

In practice investors are always trying to be just ahead of the pack in spotting and acting on the turning points. This means that, by the time a turning point is confirmed, the markets will already have moved and be looking for the next development. It also means, of course, that the markets frequently move too soon and have to reverse. It has been said in the US for example that the stock market has forecast five out of the last three recessions!

Given the difficulties just described, market timing merits a health warning (or perhaps it should be wealth warning) for the investor! Most professional investors use it very cautiously. Many do adjust the weightings of portfolios to favour bonds or stocks, or interest-sensitive stocks versus growth stocks according to their perception of the cycle, but only to a limited degree. Or if they are investing across a range of countries most will maintain a well-diversified portfolio even while overweighting their favourites. Some investors do not even attempt market timing.

Investing in themes

The alternative use of economic analysis for the investor is to invest in themes or according to views of long term trends. An obvious example is emerging markets where many investors believe that investor returns will continue to be strong over the long term because of continuing rapid economic growth.

Another example might be the view that inflation is set to stay low for the long term. Hence even though it may still rise during the late stages of economic upswing the peak will be 3-4% in most countries rather than the 5-10% levels or higher often seen in the 1970's and 1980's. This view makes bonds an attractive long term investment.

Another example would be the view that Italy will eventually find the political strength to deal with its budget and debt problems without inflation or restructuring. This would make Italian bonds an attractive long term investment.

Organisation of the book

Chapters 1-7 look at aspects of the economy and try to bring out the interactions between economic development and the markets, both in a short term business cycle sense and in terms of long term trends. Chapter 8 moves into finance theory to outline the latest academic thinking on how to invest and the practical lessons that may be drawn. Chapters 9-12 then look at the four main markets that the investor has to deal with, currencies, bonds, stocks and commodities.

While the order of chapters contains a reasonable logic each chapter can be read independently. The glossary at the end of the book provides a brief explanation of various pieces of jargon used by economists and refers the reader to the chapter where it comes up the most.

1. Economic Growth

Overview

Trend versus cycle
Measures of growth
Four ways to analyse GDP
Why do some countries grow faster than others?
Economic growth and investors

Defining GDP

Why is it called GDP?
Calculating GDP in practice

Four Ways to Analyse GDP

1. Nominal versus real GDP
2. The demand components approach
3. Investment and productivity
4. Supply of growth

Overview

Economic growth can be split into a cycle and an underlying trend. Countries with a higher trend growth rate tend to offer higher stock market returns but may have relatively high inflation and high interest rates, both in nominal and real terms. The best overall measure of economic growth is gross domestic product or GDP although other indicators of economic activity are often released earlier. In practice, although GDP is intended to be a measure of total output it has to be calculated from limited information. Four different ways of analysing GDP each provide useful insights for investors. Distinguishing nominal from real GDP and the demand components approach are sometimes called "demand side" approaches and are most often used to analyse the cycle. Distinguishing investment from productivity as sources of growth and analysing supply-side components, both "supply side" approaches, are useful for looking at trends.

Economic growth is at the heart of economics since it is growth which provides higher incomes and higher living standards. Indeed our economic and political system is so much based on continuing growth that, without it, political and social stability could be in danger. For the investor, faster economic growth is linked to higher returns which is the main reason why emerging markets have become popular with investors.

More fundamentally, economic growth is what distinguishes investment from gambling. Games of pure chance such as roulette as well as games that incorporate skills, such as poker or backing horses, suffer from the limitation that each person's winnings are offset by someone else's losses. In economics jargon, they are "zero-sum games", i.e. the sum of everybody's gains and losses is zero. Investment is different. With investment, everyone can gain, but this is true only as long as the economy continues to grow.

Trend versus cycle

For as long as economics has been a subject of study economic growth has moved in cycles, with periods of fast growth interspersed with periods of slow growth or decline. Economists like to separate this cycle from the "trend" or "underlying" growth of the economy *(see chart over page)*. The advantage of this approach is that it divides the study of economic growth into two disciplines, an analysis of the cycle and an analysis of the trend (the subject of this chapter). Chapter 2 looks at business cycles. Incidentally, while it is convenient to split growth into two components like this, it should not be assumed that the trend is completely independent of the cycle. Some economists argue that a long period of recession may actually depress the trend rate of growth and vice versa. The chart shows GDP growth since 1962 for the industrial countries. Since the early 1970s the cycle has become more pronounced while trend growth has declined.

GDP Growth in Industrial Countries

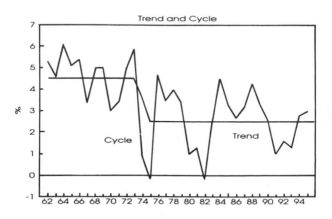

Measures of growth

Economists measure the output or production of an economy with a variety of measures but *gross domestic product (GDP)* is now the most commonly used. GDP measures the total value of goods and services produced in an economy, i.e. everything produced for sale. For the investor, while GDP is always the most important ultimate measure, the data are usually released comparatively late. Other data releases which give partial clues to the direction of the economy are often focused on more closely because they give an earlier indication. *Industrial production* is one such key indicator. Although industry accounts for only around 25% of GDP in most OECD countries its output tends to be more volatile than the rest of the economy and therefore it provides a good signal of trends in the overall economy. When the economy is expanding producers will often increase output faster than sales in anticipation of future sales (not wanting to miss out and not fearful of being left with unsold inventory). When the economy is contracting industrial production will often decline much more than GDP because producers are trying to clear excess inventories. Other useful indicators of the direction of GDP are *employment*, *retail sales* and *consumer spending*.

Four ways to analyse GDP

For investors there are four different ways that GDP can be analysed, each of which provides useful insights.

1. Nominal versus real GDP. The difference between the two is inflation, in this case as measured by the *GDP price deflator*. Real GDP is what counts and what can be compared across countries and across time.

2. The demand components approach. This looks at the various components of GDP, e.g. *consumer spending, investment, government spending,* etc. Each of these components responds in different ways to changes in variables such as interest rates, and exchange rates and so economist use this breakdown as a way of analysing the likel changes in the economy.

3. Investment versus productivity. How mu the increase in output is due to new machines which can create more output (i.e. new inves and how much is due to better use of the existing machines, (i.e. greater productivity)?

4. Supply-side components of growth. Growth is broken down into changes in employment and changes in labour productivity. These four approaches are analysed in detail later in this chapter. Note that another way of breaking down GDP by components is to look at the income side, although this is less commonly used. On the income side gross domestic income is equal to wages, profits, dividends on shares and interest. A third way is to look at total sales of goods and services.

Why do some countries grow faster than others?

The simplest way to answer this question is in terms of the third approach to GDP discussed above, namely investment and productivity, i.e. output per man-hour. The fast-growing countries of Asia have all had relatively high investment rates and high productivity growth rates.

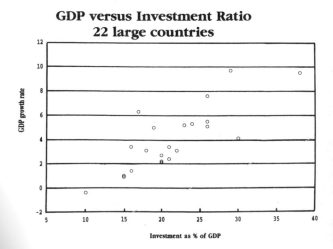

GDP versus Investment Ratio 22 large countries

at determines how high investment and vity rates are? Rates of investment are closely related to the level of savings. If current spending on goods and services is high, perhaps because wages are high or consumer borrowings are high or because the government is running a large budget deficit, then there are less resources available for investment. If the economy is generating higher savings then it is more likely, though by no means certain, to go into investment for increasing capacity. It might for example go into housing or into financing a government deficit or into investments overseas.

How can countries generate higher savings? One way is for governments to reduce budget deficits or even generate surpluses. Studies of the successful East Asian countries show that budget surpluses have been an important factor in their success. The other way is to encourage private savings. In the East Asian countries private savings are high partly because there is very little in the way of a government safety net for unemployment or old age. For the developed countries most studies focus on the desirability of reducing taxation on savings, e.g. reducing taxes on interest from deposits and capital gains.

GDP: Long-Term Growth Rate

%	1970s	Rank	1980s	Rank
Korea	9.6	1	9.6	1
Egypt	9.5	2	4.8	6
Brazil	8.1	3	2.5	11
Indonesia	7.2	4	5.6	4
Thailand	7.1	5	7.9	2
Pakistan	4.9	6	6.1	3
Japan	4.3	7	4.2	7
India	3.4	8	5.4	5
France	3.2	9	2.3	12
USA	2.8	10	2.6	10
Germany	2.6	11	2.3	13
UK	2.0	12	2.9	9
Chile	1.4	13	3.6	8

Source: World Bank

High productivity growth is linked to a whole ho of factors including good education and training flexible trades unions, competition, dynamic entrepreneurship, moderate taxes, work ethics and of course high investment itself.

Economic growth and investors

Short term changes in the rate of economic growth are crucial for investors because they influence interest rate policy and company performance, which in turn feed through to the markets. This is the subject of chapter 2 of this series, which looks at the business cycle. Long term trends in GDP growth are important to investors for three reasons.

Firstly, countries with a higher trend growth rate usually show strong returns on stocks because profits rise at a rapid pace. Of course the markets anticipate this growth and therefore usually value high growth countries at high price-earnings ratios. Still, returns will be high provided that the high growth continues.

Secondly, high growth countries tend to have higher inflation as the strong growth puts demand pressures on sectors of the economy such as infrastructure and skilled labour. *Thirdly,* they will usually have higher interest rates, both at the short and the long end. This is partly due to the high inflation and partly because high growth requires high investment which puts upward pressure on interest rates.

Defining GDP

Why is it called GDP?

GDP is called *gross* domestic product because it includes the investment made to replace the machines that wear out in the process of producing that output. Since we do not know how quickly things really do wear out or become obsolete the calculation of net domestic product (i.e. after subtracting replacement investment) is dubious though that does not stop the statisticians). It is d *domestic* product to distinguish it from al product (as in GNP) which is sometimes used. Domestic product is all production within a country while national product is all production by the nationals of a country, including those working abroad.

The way GDP is defined makes it equal to gross income as well as to gross spending. Clearly the total value of goods and services bought must be equal to the total value sold. In turn, these must also be equal to total incomes, including wages, profits, interest and rents.

Note that GDP is calculated on an "added value" basis. In other words the statisticians have to avoid any double counting such as including both the overall value of a new car and the value of its steel and tyres.

Calculating GDP in practice

The precision in the statistics makes GDP look like a very accurate number. The reality of course is that it is no more than the best guess that can be made. In practice, figures are based on very sketchy data. Obviously the government statisticians cannot add up all the value of the output of the economy or indeed all the incomes or all the spending every quarter. They simply do not have all the information. What they do is make a major computation every few years using all the available data including income tax returns, sales tax returns and business and retail sales figures. In between they rely on the use of data that is available monthly to build up a picture which it is hoped will approximate the real GDP. One drawback of this approach is that periodically past GDP data are revised substantially when the big survey comes up with a new set of numbers.

Four Ways to Analyse GDP

1. Nominal versus real GDP

The distinction between nominal and real GD' basic but crucial. The difference between th inflation, in this case a measure called the GDP price deflator. It is called a "deflator" because it pricks the balloon of rising prices and deflates the nominal figures on output, bringing them back to the real increase in goods and services output. Calculations are made as to how much of the nominal rise is due to price changes and how much due to volume changes. However, since it is difficult to judge inflation effects, the calculation is subject to considerable doubt.

For example, suppose we know that the price of a Porsche 911 has risen 35% in the last ten years. We could conclude that this is all inflation, but Porsche would undoubtedly argue otherwise, citing improved features and options that are now fitted as standard. How much of the rise in price is due to extra real value and how much is down to inflation? The statisticians have to make these decisions and they would be the first to admit that there are lots of questions over the calculations. This is particularly true the longer the period. For example the Porsche 911 usually does not change much from quarter to quarter, but over ten years it will be a significantly different car. Fortunately, for the investor the long term is not all that important. The main question is whether the economy is growing at a fast pace or a slow pace, and the data generally are good enough for that.

2. The demand components approach

The Demand Components approach (economists also call it the Keynesian approach) looks at GDP by analysing the various components of demand, economists' jargon for spending. This is the way that the statisticians calculate GDP numbers and it is also the way that most economists try to forecast it. Note that each component has to be measured in real terms, i.e. after stripping out inflation.

Each of these components responds in different ways to changes in variables such as interest rates, government spending and exchange rates and so economists use this breakdown as a way of analysing the likely changes in the economy. For example consumer spending depends primarily on income but also on such factors as consumer confidence, interest rates, house prices, etc. The following sections look at this breakdown in detail.

GDP by Component: United States 1994

US $ billion	Value	% of total
a. Consumption	**4627**	**69**
durable goods	591	9
non-durable goods	1394	21
services	2642	39
b. Gross private domestic investment	**1038**	**15**
fixed investment	980	14
business	698	10
residential	282	4
c. Change in inventories	**58**	**1**
d. Net exports	**-102**	**-1**
exports	716	11
imports	818	12
Government spending	**1174**	**17**
Gross Domestic Product	**6737**	**100**

Source: Table 1.1 US Survey of Current Business

a. Consumer spending: Data are published on retail sales broken down into durable and non-durable goods, car sales and, after a delay, consumer spending. Retail sales (which in the USA includes car sales but not in the UK data) is the best overall number. Durable goods and car sales are good indicators of consumer confidence since in recession it is the big-ticket items and especially cars on which consumers cut back. Then there are the indicators which feed into consumers' spending decisions such as real wages (i.e. wage growth after inflation), employment trends (rising employment both increases consumer income and improves confidence), the rate of interest and consumer confidence.

The effect of the rate of interest varies from country to country. In the UK short term inte rates have been very important because of the prevalence of floating rate mortgages. Lower interest rates immediately impact on consumers because they have lower mortgage payments. In other countries the effect of falling short term interest rates is less certain because lower rates reduce consumers' spending because of the fall in interest income. Bond yields are more important in the United States where mortgages are usually at fixed rates.

Consumer Spending Indicators

Measures	Influences
Consumer expenditure	Income growth
Retail sales	Consumer confidence
Car sales	Unemployment
Department store sales	House prices
	Interest rates

b. Investment: The key measures are capital goods orders and business investment as reported in the GDP breakdown. Monthly or even quarterly data are not given too much attention because they are extremely volatile. But even though business investment is only around 15-20% of GDP in most countries, it tends to move up and down more strongly than consumer spending and therefore is very important for the cycle. The key inputs to forecasting business spending are the level of capacity utilisation, the rate of growth of sales and the rate of interest. Again countries vary as to the relative importance of short term rates and bond yelds. In Germany and Japan long rates are more important while in the UK short rates are key. The and France fall in between. Related to all these he state of corporate balance sheets. When anies are over-extended with debt they will ly respond more quickly to higher interest a downturn in demand.

Business Investment Indicators

Measures	Influences
Fixed investment	Sales
Capital goods orders	Interest rates
Purchasing Managers reports (US, UK)	Capacity utilisation
Inventories	Business confidence
	GDP growth

c. Business spending on inventories: This is important primarily because of its role in the business cycle *(see chapter 2)*. Expectations of rising demand will prompt companies to order more goods or produce more, and this extra production creates jobs and incomes which, for the economy as a whole, makes sure that the extra demand does indeed come through. Interpreting inventories behaviour though, is always awkward. For example, suppose the government reports a rise in inventories. Is this due to business anticipating a rise in demand or in fact due to levels of sales lower than hoped, giving an involuntary rise in inventories?

d. Exports and imports: The key factors behind exports and imports are the exchange rate and the relative speed of GDP growth in the home and foreign countries. Fast growth at home tends to crimp exports because manufacturers are less inclined to bid keenly for foreign contracts when they are busy with the home market. Faster growth abroad obviously makes it easier to export.

To calculate GDP the statisticians use a concept called "net exports" which is exports less imports. Note that if exports rise rapidly but imports rise equally fast there is no net contribution to GDP. Trade data are important for what they reveal about the contribution to economic growth from trade. Ideally the breakdown is provided according to volume and price, since otherwise it is very diffi to reach much of a conclusion.

3. Investment and productivity

The third way of breaking down GDP growth is to separate it into new output due to new investment and new output due to productivity growth. In other words how much of the increase in output is due to new machines which can create more output and how much is due to better use of the existing machines?

In reality this can never be reliably measured because so often what happens is that output rises because the old machines are replaced. The new machines are not adding to capacity but in fact allow more productivity growth. Nevertheless the distinction is very important conceptually. As with an individual company, countries must invest a certain amount each year just to repair and replace old machinery. It is only when investment goes above that level that new capacity is created enabling the economy to produce more goods. Hence economists often look at the ratio of investment to GDP. If that ratio is only in the area of 10% then the chances are that most of the investment is simply repairing worn out machinery. If, however, like Japan and many of the Asian newly industrialising countries, the ratio is around 30% or more, then there is a substantial amount of new capacity being created.

However, high investment does not necessarily mean faster GDP growth. Faster growth depends on the new plant or equipment being used effectively. Hence, the need to look at the productivity of that investment. Here again the Asian countries often show particularly high productivity on new investment whereas other countries often show it lower. We are here referring to labour productivity, i.e. the output per man hour.

Supply of growth

final way of analysing GDP looks at the
onents of growth on the supply side. The
st way to look at this is to divide growth into

changes in employment and changes in labour productivity. Sometimes for longer term analysis this is broken down further into changes in the labour force, changes in labour force participation (e.g. more or less women or older people working) and labour productivity.

For example US GDP growth is conventionally thought to be likely to average 2½% per annum over the next 10 years which is based on just under a 1% growth of the labour force, a small rise in labour force participation and a rise in labour productivity annually of about 1%. If productivity were to rise then GDP could grow faster too. In contrast the figures for some of the Asian countries would be more like 2% labour force growth, 1% p.a. from increased participation and 5-6% from productivity.

2. Business Cycles

Overview

A Typical Business Cycle Described

Phase I recovery
Phase II early upswing
Phase III late upswing
Phase IV economy slows or goes into recession
Phase V recession

Investment and the Cycle

Two approaches for investors
The role of leading indicators

Key Aspects of the Cycle

How do depressions fit in?
Why does the cycle exist?
Where does the recovery come from?

The 1982-91 Cycle in the USA

Kondratieff Cycles

Five Phases of the Business Cycle

I. Recovery
- Stimulatory economic policies
- Confidence picks up
- Inflation still falling

MARKETS ... short rates falling, bond yields bottoming, stocks rising, commodities rising

II. Early Upswing
- Increasing confidence
- Healthy economic growth
- Inflation remains low

MARKETS ... short rates bottoming, bonds stable, stocks and commodities strong

III. Late Upswing
- Boom mentality
- Inflation gradually picks up
- Policy becomes restrictive

MARKETS ... short rates rising, bond yields rise, stocks topping out, commodity prices rising strongly

IV. Economy slows or enters Recession
- Short term interest rates peak
- Confidence drops suddenly
- Inventory correction begins
- Inflation continues to accelerate

MARKETS ... short rates peak, bond yields top out, stocks fall, commodity prices fall

V. Recession
- Production falling
- Inflation peaks
- Confidence weak

MARKETS ... short rates drop, bond yields drop, stocks rising, commodities weak

Overview

The business cycle can be broadly described in terms of 5 phases: Recovery, early upswing, late upswing, slowing economy, recession. Inflation tends to lag the economic cycle by a year or more. Stocks do best in recession, recovery and early upswing while bonds do best rather earlier. But, in practice, market timing is not easy.

Business cycles have been documented at least since the 18th century and seem to be an inescapable feature of the market economy. Periodically, usually near the height of an economic boom people begin to argue that business cycles have been abolished, but, so far, every upswing has ended in recession and every recession has given way to recovery. Business cycles are crucial for investors, most of whom spend a great deal of time trying to guess when the next turning point is coming. In practice the length of the cycle, the strength of the upswing and the depth of the recession vary considerably and are impossible to predict accurately. Nevertheless for investors, being aware of the pattern is crucial.

 In the simplest terms the business cycle (sometimes called *trade cycle*) is an alternation of periods of faster growth with periods of slower growth or declines. However many analysts believe that there is more than one cycle. In a famous, and famously long book, Joseph Schumpeter writing in 1939 argued that there are 3 cycles. There is a three-year cycle, which he called the Kitchin cycle (after another economist Joseph Kitchin). Then there is a nine-year cycle called the Juglar cycle (another economist) and finally a very long cycle the Kondratieff cycle (a Russian economist, see below). However, since the Second World War, short cycles appear to have lasted anywhere between 2.5 and nine years while the existence of the nine-year cycle was in doubt during the 1950s and 1960s. Few believe that the cycle can be predicted with regularity. Despite exhaustive attempts it remains elusive: a great deal is known about patterns of cycles but it has proved difficult to use this information in a predictive way because every cycle is different.

A Typical Business Cycle Described

The following is a description of the usual course of a business cycle which can apply as well to a short cycle of 3-4 years or a long cycle of 9 years or more. The very long term Kondratieff cycle is discussed in more detail separately below. The comments on what the markets are doing at each phase need to be treated carefully. In a sense the markets are always adjusting to new views on how long the current phase is going to last or how strong it will be, when the next phase will begin and how long that will last. Remember that cycles since the early 1970s have been more pronounced than in the first decades after the Second World War, with deeper recessions.

Phase I recovery

This is usually a short phase of a few months in which the economy picks up from its slowdown or recession. Note that recoveries are often not seen as such until several months after they really happen. The same goes for the onset of recession and is a reflection of the delays in economic data. In the recovery phase there are often stimulatory economic policies from the government in the form of lower interest rates or a fiscal stimulus. Note that these policy measures normally influence the economy with a lag of a few months and continue to provide stimulus for at least a year in the case of interest rates and around 2 years in the case of fiscal policy. Generally confidence is picking up among businesses and usually among consumers.

A crucial factor supporting the recovery is usually the inventory cycle whereby renewed confidence prompts business to increase inventories in anticipation of higher sales and the process of doing so generates income and jobs in the economy. There may be an expansion of investment with new products and new processes. Sometimes the stimulus can come from abroad with fast growth elsewhere giving good export growth. This was the case for example for Germany in 1982-3 when the rapid pace of the US expansion provided a convenient locomotive. In this phase unemployment may still be rising, or at least not falling yet, but overtime work will be increasing. Inflation, which tends to cycle with the economic cycle a year or so behind, will still be falling.

USA: Recoveries and the Stock Market

| Cycle | | Return from the S&P Index* | |
Peak	Trough	Trough Year	Following Year
Aug. 1929	Mar. 1933	53.0	-1.5
May 1937	June 1938	30.0	-0.8
Feb. 1945	Oct. 1945	35.7	-7.8
Nov. 1948	Oct. 1949	17.8	30.5
July 1953	May 1954	51.2	31.0
Aug. 1957	Apr. 1958	42.4	11.8
Apr. 1960	Feb. 1961	26.6	-8.8
Dec. 1969	Nov. 1970	3.5	14.1
Nov. 1973	Mar. 1975	36.9	23.6
Jan. 1980	July 1980	31.5	-4.8
July 1981	Nov. 1982	20.5	22.3
July 1990	Mar. 1991	30.0	7.4

* Price appreciation plus dividends

Source: National Bureau of Economic Research and Standard & Poor's Security Price Index Record

In the markets, short term interest rates may still be falling as the government tries to ensure the recovery continues. Inflation will be down and unemployment up so the government may well be concentrating mainly on making sure that recovery takes hold. Bond yields may continue to come down through this phase but are likely to be bottoming. The crucial factor here is the strength of the recovery. Stock markets may rise strongly at this point because fears of a longer recession or depression dissipate. Cyclical stocks should do well. Commodity prices rise strongly too, especially for industrial commodities.

Phase II early upswing

The recovery period is past, confidence is up and the economy is gaining some momentum. This is the healthiest period of the cycle in a sense, because economic growth can be healthy without any signs of *overheating* or sharply higher inflation. Typically there is a virtuous circle of increasing confidence with consumers prepared to borrow and spend more and business, facing increased capacity use, keen to invest. Unemployment falls, usually rapidly in countries like the United States where the recession prompts temporary lay-offs but more slowly in Europe. Higher operating levels allow many businesses to enjoy a fall in unit costs so that profits rise. Inflation may pick up off the bottom because cut-throat price competition eases as sales pick up, but only rises slowly.

In the markets short rates bottom at this time and central banks may begin to edge them up, while further up the yield curve interest rates are likely to be stable or to be rising slightly. Stocks are strong with recovery stocks in particular doing well at this stage, while commodity prices are probably moving up gently. This phase usually lasts at least a year and often for several years.

Phase III late upswing

This is where the boom mentality has taken hold, as for example in many countries at the end of the 1980s. The economy grows rapidly, capacity utilisation nears a peak prompting an investment boom and unemployment falls. Property prices and rents often move up strongly at this stage prompting a construction boom. Inflation picks up, usually slowly at first with wages accelerating too as shortages of labour develop.

In the markets, typically interest rates are rising as the monetary authorities become restrictive to try to slow the boom down, while heavy borrowing puts pressure on the credit markets. Bond markets anxiously watch this behaviour and usually bond yields will be rising. Stock markets may be nervous too, depending on the strength of the boom and this is not usually the best time for stocks. Commodity prices are liable to soar as capacity limits are reached and, at the same time, investors looking for a hedge against inflation take speculative positions.

Phase IV economy slows or goes into recession

At this point the economy is declining but usually, because of the lags in reporting, recession is not confirmed until at least three months after it began. For example the 1990 US recession is now dated as beginning in July 1990, (just before Saddam Hussein invaded Kuwait), but was not widely seen as occurring until October/November of that year. Typically, short term interest rates move up sharply and then peak when confidence drops rather suddenly for some reason. The slowdown is exacerbated by the inventory correction as companies, suddenly fearing recession, try to reduce their inventory levels. At this point, capacity utilisation begins to drop off but wages move on ahead since labour markets are still tight, with the result that inflation continues to rise. Inflation usually peaks around a year into recession.

In the markets short term rates peak and then begin to fall. How quickly they fall depends on how long the monetary authorities want to keep the squeeze on to reduce inflation. Bond yields top out and start to fall. The stock market may fall, perhaps significantly, with interest sensitive stocks including utilities doing best. Commodity prices top out and may fall.

Phase V recession

Once the recession is confirmed monetary policy is usually eased but often cautiously at first. Moreover there is always a lag between cuts in interest rates and recovery. Recessions typically last 6 months to a year. Both consumer and business confidence is weak. The mistakes of the boom have come home to roost with individuals and companies likely to find themselves with assets worth much less than they thought and debts which are difficult to service. In a severe recession the financial system may have a serious problem with bad debts, which makes lenders extremely cautious. The inventory correction is in full flow and as long as it continues will tend to keep the economy in recession. Unemployment rises fast which starts to put downward pressure on inflation.

In the markets short term interest rates drop during this phase as do bond yields. Depending on how badly confidence is affected stock markets may fall precipitously at first in response to reports of company losses and bankruptcies but then recover on the back of lower interest rates and hopes for economic recovery. Commodity prices are weak as surplus capacity opens up.

Investment and the Cycle

The description of a typical cycle above makes investment sound easy. Just buy stocks once the recession is underway and buy bonds at the peak of the boom! In practice market timing is much more difficult because each cycle varies in length and amplitude (height of the boom and depth of the recession). Investors are often afraid of buying too soon or selling too late. Moreover since the overall pattern is well known everybody else is trying to move just ahead of the market. This is one reason why the stock market is seen as a leading indicator of the economy. Investors try to jump in and out before the economy turns.

For example in 1986-7 investors felt that the

cyclical upswing could last much longer than normal and therefore were comfortable, until the Summer of 1987 with the run-up in the market. In a recession confidence is usually low and investors worry that the outlook can become much darker. In late 1990 the worry was that the conflict with Iraq could keep oil prices high for a long time and might not go well. Even if there are not political factors like this it is often easy to argue that a recession is going to get worse before it gets better and in the darkest hour there is often much talk of depression.

Two approaches for investors

For investors there are two ways to approach the business cycle. One is to attempt to spot the turning points and shift asset allocation between bonds, stocks and cash accordingly. But in practice this is very difficult. The danger is not just that the portfolio may be too heavy on stocks when stock prices fall but that it may be too light when they rise. Most professional investors only change their asset weighting within certain limits and always keep a core of bonds and stocks in their portfolios.

The second approach is to ignore the business cycle and concentrate on picking good companies. This is a longer-term approach, looking through the business cycle rather than trying to forecast it. Many professionals use a combination of both approaches.

The role of leading indicators

To identify where we are in the business cycle economists rely heavily on leading indicators and business survey results.

The leading indicators index in most countries is an average of around a dozen indicators which, historically, have been found to lead the business cycle by a few months. However the lead time varies considerably, for example in the USA, from as low as one or two months up to 18 months or more. Several of the components of the index (*see below*) are watched particularly closely, for example, weekly unemployment claims, new orders and consumer confidence.

Note that employment is not a leading indicator but a coincident indicator, i.e. it is in line with the cycle. Its popularity as an indicator, particularly in the US is twofold. Firstly, the employment report does in fact contain a wealth of other information including hours worked and wages. Secondly, it is reported only 3-4 weeks after the survey is taken. Hence for example, the February employment report (based on a survey near the beginning of the month) will be released at the beginning of March. Later in March the January index of leading indicators will be published.

US Leading Indicators

Weekly hours in manufacturing
Weekly new unemployment claims
Manufacturers' new orders
Vendor performance (Deliveries index)
Orders for plant and equipment
Change in manufacturers' unfilled orders
Housing permits
Change in sensitive materials prices
Index of stock prices
Money supply M2
Index of Consumer Expectations (University of Michigan)

Source: Commerce Department

Key Aspects of the Cycle

How do depressions fit in?

The word depression is usually understood to mean a slump in output of 10% or more, with a massive rise in unemployment. This was the experience in the 1930s, especially in the United States. Since the Second World War downturns have usually been described as recessions, which is partly euphemistic but also reflects that, at least until the 1970s, downturns were very mild. The typical post war recession has resulted in drops in output of between 2-4% and rises in the unemployment rate of a similar order. There are probably two reasons for this.

First governments now play a very active role in re-stimulating an economy which is in recession. They safeguard the banking system to avoid the kind of collapse seen in the USA in the 1930s. They often use one or both of fiscal and monetary policy to kick-start the economy. Not only does this directly end the recession but it also influences expectations so that the blind fear that was seen in the early 1930s is ruled out. Perhaps the extreme recent example is Japan in 1992-95 which used active fiscal policy, active monetary policy, implicit support for banks and direct stock market support to try to ensure that the economy did not go into too deep a recession.

The *second* factor is that the economy is more resilient to major recessions or depressions now because the public sector itself is so much larger. In most countries the public sector is 40% of GDP and spending there changes only slowly in the event of a recession. The serious downward spiral seen in the early 1930s is therefore more muted. The so-called automatic stabilisers ensure that the government's budget deficit opens up automatically in a recession providing a source of demand which partially counteracts the private sector's lack of spending.

Why does the cycle exist?

Explanations put forward vary from theories related to sun spots (which were thought to influence agriculture) to sophisticated mathematical models based on expectations and investment behaviour. Probably the best way to look at this question is to ask why booms end and why (some time later) recoveries begin.

There are broadly three types of factors that seem to bring the boom to an end. *First*, there are the inherent or natural economic factors in the cyclical situation. For example consumers may be relatively satiated with new cars and consumer goods and decide to rein in their borrowings. Another possibility is that after a boom in investment, companies suddenly find themselves with excess capacity and cut back. Another factor can be that prices rise too far and people hold back on spending. However, sometimes while these factors may be present they are not the triggering factor which ends a boom and takes the economy into the recession. The *second* type of factor is some sort of shock to the system from a political event such as a war or perhaps a rise in oil prices. The last three recessions have involved the dramatic move in oil prices although, as mentioned above, the 1990 US recession did in fact begin just before Saddam Hussein's invasion of Kuwait. The *third* factor is government policy primarily in the form of monetary factors. The monetary authorities deliberately bring booms to an end because they want to rein in inflation. They may intend or at least announce that they intend to engineer a slowdown or a *soft landing* but, as illustrated very effectively in the 1980s, it is very difficult to fine-tune the economy. The cynic has often seen the timing of this monetary policy as being linked to elections. This has been especially noticeable in countries where the government controls monetary policy directly as was the case in the UK until 1993.

Where does the recovery come from?

During a recession it is often very hard to see where the recovery is going to come from. Who is going to start spending again when all around everything is depressed?. Typically there are four important factors. *Firstly*, the government is likely to be actively stimulating the economy. Lower interest rates encourage spending and borrowing and also lower the burden of existing debt. Fiscal policy directly puts more money into the economy. *Secondly*, during the recession consumers and business are actively reducing debts. This is often what keeps the recession going. At some point, with the help of lower interest rates, they may become more relaxed about borrowing. *Thirdly*, asset prices fall during the recession, eventually to the point where people are prepared to buy again. *Finally*, the inventory cycle plays a key role.

The 1982-91 Cycle in the USA

The following description treats the period as one (comparatively) long cycle. Some analysts would break it up into two sub-cycles reflecting the growth pause in 1986.

Phase 1 recovery: The recovery began in the fourth quarter of 1982 though, as usual, it was not evident until a few months later. It came as a result of a massive fiscal stimulus put into place by President Reagan in the form of lower taxes and higher defence spending. Also interest rates came down sharply from August 1982, (partly in response to the Mexican debt default). Initially inventories played a big role in leading demand.

In the markets, interest rates fell until early in 1983, bond yields fell with them and then stabilised, while stock prices rose strongly.

US Cycle: 1981-93

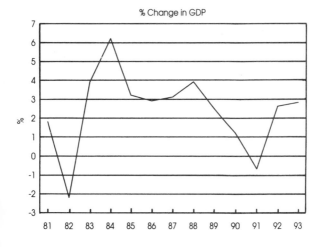

% Change in GDP

Phase 2 early upswing: This was a strong recovery with GDP growth averaging 5% in 1983-4, quickly taking the economy back to the unemployment rate of 7% seen immediately before the recession. In the markets, the strength of the recovery encouraged the Federal Reserve to raise interest rates and bond yields rose too. The stock market paused before moving up again from 1985 onwards. Inflation stayed very modest in the early 1980s, partly helped by the rise in the dollar.

This phase lasted much longer than normal, probably for two reasons. One was that the 1980-2 slowdown had been particularly long and drawn out, which left scope for a longer upswing. Secondly, and most importantly, oil prices fell by around half in 1986, sharply reducing inflationary pressures world-wide and allowing interest rates to fall.

Phase 3 late upswing: This phase can be dated from early 1987. After the pause in growth in 1986 the economy started to accelerate again. Confidence rose sharply, helped by low interest rates and the massive devaluation of the dollar. The low rate of inflation (following the oil price decline) encouraged the view that the upswing still had a long way to go. In fact it was at this time that a few articles appeared pronouncing the business cycle dead!

Unemployment began to drop steadily, passing through 6%, which started to ring warning bells at the Fed and then on to 5%. Inflation began to edge up again.

In the markets stocks of course boomed in the first half of 1987, crashed and then gradually made their way to new peaks by 1989. Bond yields rose sharply in early 1987 but then took comfort from the stock market crash which seemed to point to recession and the tightening stance of the Federal Reserve. Commodity prices rose strongly.

Phase 4 slowdown into recession: The avowed aim of the Federal Reserve was a "soft landing" and the economy slowed down nicely in 1989 and into 1990. The Federal Reserve began to cut Fed funds rate in the second quarter of 1989 and the economy bounced along at a slow rate. In the first few months of 1990 employment and consumer confidence weakened as did investment. Construction spending dropped off sharply, both for houses and commercial use. This combination was already taking the economy into a mild recession in the third quarter of 1990. But then came the shock, the invasion of Kuwait, the sharp rise in oil prices and the uncertainty over the outcome of the US military build-up.

Stock prices fell sharply as did bond yields. The Federal Reserve cut rates sharply. But confidence had already fallen, so spending and hiring decisions were delayed. Property prices fell and banks suddenly looked weak.

Phase 5 recession: The initial recession lasted about 9 months. Uncertainty over the Gulf crisis and oil prices combined with a classic inventory cycle to make the economy weaker. At the same time property prices were falling and consumers were worried about rising unemployment in the face of high debts. The Fed cut interest rates by 2% between November 1990 and March 1991. The economy rebounded strongly in Spring 1991 with the war successfully over. However, after the initial bounce, the economy was locked into a sluggish and hesitant growth trend until the second half of 1992, with industrial production trending up only very slightly.

In the markets stocks fell on the invasion of Kuwait and bottomed in October before starting to pick up. The beginning of the war gave stocks a sharp boost and signs of the ending of the recession in the Spring took the market higher. Bond yields peaked in September, reflecting worries about the impact of higher oil prices. Once it became clear that the economy was in recession, from about October 1990, bonds rallied, with yields dropping almost 100 basis points.

Kondratieff Cycles

In 1925 a Russian economist called Nikolai Kondratieff, published a book called "The Long Waves in Economic Life" which claimed to identify a 50-60 year long cycle. In its strict form the Kondratieff cycle is supposed to consist of a 20-25 year upswing, followed by a 20-30 year down-wave. The down-wave does not mean that the economy is in decline for the whole time, only that average growth is slower and recessions tend to be long and deep while upswings are short or mild. The theory behind the cycle is that it is due to the long life of capital goods and the tendency for periodic investment booms.

Many studies have attempted to find long cycles but few have found the regular cycle that Kondratieff claimed (based on detailed statistical studies). There is also a problem in that, given the length of the cycle, there can only be 4 cycles since the industrial revolution began in the 1780s which, for statisticians does not amount to many observations! Also, given the huge changes in the structure of economies over such long periods it seems doubtful whether the cycle would continue to remain the same length. Another criticism that is sometimes levelled is that many of the key turning points in the world economy seem to be linked to wars. But of course Kondratieff was writing in a Marxist tradition so that he saw wars not as random events but as part of the system. In fact he argued that wars normally occur in the upswing.

Nevertheless the world economic slowdown of the 1970s encouraged renewed interest in the Kondratieff cycle. In 1925 Kondratieff dated the beginning of a downswing as around 1914-20. That points to the beginning of the next downswing due 50-60 years later, in the 1970s. Later analysts dated the beginning of the upswing in that cycle as around 1940. Hence the good news is that the 1990s could see the beginning of a new upswing!

3. Inflation and Unemployment

Overview

The Phillips curve
What causes inflation?
What level of inflation is tolerable?
Why did inflation pick up in the 1960s?
Indicators of inflation

Measuring The Forces on Inflation

The output gap
The natural rate of unemployment
Why is the NAIRU not zero?

Inflation and Investors

Low inflation in the 1990s
Inflation and investment returns

Overview

Inflation and unemployment tend to move in opposite directions. When unemployment falls below a certain level inflation picks up and vice-versa. During the 1960s it was widely believed that this relationship, usually referred to as the Phillips Curve, would hold for the long term so that governments could choose to tolerate a higher level of inflation in exchange for lower unemployment. During the 1970s this policy came unstuck as countries suffered from high unemployment and inflation simultaneously. In the 1990s inflation in most countries is back to levels last seen in the 1960s.

In some ways the analysis of inflation and unemployment is another way of looking at the business cycle. During recessions, unemployment rises and inflation tends to fall, while during the boom unemployment falls and inflation rises. But it is worth analysing these two aspects in more detail both to understand the timing of the cycle and to look at the long term trends in inflation which have played such a crucial role in determining investment returns since the early 1970s.

The Phillips curve

The idea that there is a fixed relationship between inflation and unemployment was suggested by an economist called A. W. H. Phillips in 1957. He plotted the unemployment rate against the inflation rate for 100 years of UK data and showed that high inflation was associated with low unemployment and vice versa. This plot became known as the Phillips Curve. During the 1960s the Phillips curve became the subject of an enormous amount of economic analysis and discussion. The question, which was debated endlessly, was whether governments could choose where they wanted the economy to be on this curve. For example could governments choose to accept a slightly higher level of inflation and thereby achieve lower unemployment? Many economists thought so in the early 1960s.

However, in the late 1960s and 1970s both inflation and unemployment rose to higher levels and it became clear that such a choice does not exist over the long run. The chart below shows a plot of the Phillips Curve for the US economy for each year since 1960. It shows how the economy has moved up and down a short run curve for each movement (nearly) always showing higher inflation when unemployment falls or vice-versa. The whole curve moved up in the 1970s and early 1980s but seems to have moved down again since the mid-1980s.

Governments can stimulate the economy to achieve a lower rate of unemployment, and inflation will naturally rise. But after a while the economy slows and unemployment rises. It is now generally believed that over time the level of inflation is independent of the rate of unemployment. This does not alter the short term observation that a rise in unemployment will lower inflation, but it does mean that ultimately it is no use accepting a higher rate of inflation and hoping that this will give a permanently lower rate of unemployment. It was this realisation that led to a revolt against Keynesian economics in the 1970s and also lay behind the strong drive in the 1980s to reduce inflation.

No Long Run Phillips Curve

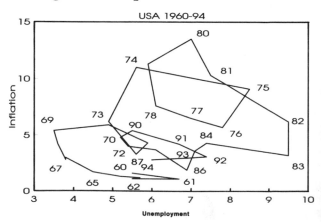

What causes inflation?

In looking at the causes of inflation, economists have traditionally divided into two camps. One, the monetarist camp, sees a growth in the money supply as the cause of inflation by pushing up demand for goods and labour. The other looks for the causes of inflation in supply and demand for goods and labour which is then accommodated by rising money supply. The monetarist approach is generally out of favour with policy-makers now, with the possible exception of the Bundesbank. The problem is that the relationship between money and inflation has proved to be unstable and unpredictable in recent years, particularly in the short term. With monetarism very much in the background, attention now focuses more on the supply and demand for goods in the economy.

Inflation is like a heavy moving vehicle with a great deal of momentum. It takes a lot to slow it down or speed it up. For example suppose inflation is at 5% and workers are used to obtaining 7% in annual wage negotiations. It will usually require a sharp rise in unemployment to reduce that wage growth to say 4% but this will only gradually produce a drop in inflation. The rise in unemployment required, especially if labour markets are not very flexible or if unions are strong, may be substantial. Very often price inflation is slow to respond to lower wage growth because the context is one of economic slowdown, when business costs per unit of output are rising and companies may at first try to raise margins.

At any one time a particular level of inflation, whether 2% or 5%, tends to be built into the system. The key question for the markets is whether the balance of forces in the economy is making inflation slow down or accelerate.

What level of inflation is tolerable?

When analysing likely government policy, investors need to make a judgement on what level of inflation is likely to be seen as acceptable by the government and by the electorate. For example, experience suggests that the United States and the UK have a higher tolerance of inflation than Germany. The reason for this is well known. Germany has suffered two major hyperinflations this century and Germans are afraid that even inflation at the 4-5% level could lead to another hyperinflation. In contrast, in the US and UK, once inflation moves below about 4%, concern focuses on the level of unemployment.

Some countries, notably New Zealand and Canada, have changed in the last 10 years to be much more intolerant of inflation than previously. Giving independence to Central Banks is often a signal that policy on inflation will be much tougher. Nevertheless if governments want to reduce inflation the only sure way is to engineer an economic slowdown or recession, which means a rise in unemployment.

Why did inflation pick up in the 1960s?

Except during wartime, price inflation during the 19th century and through the 20th century until the 1960s was negligible. Indeed the price level in the UK fell for a large part of the 19th century. The period of relatively high inflation between the 1960s and 1980s is therefore an unusual period historically. A number of reasons for this have been put forward.

An obvious point is that in fact there was a war, the Vietnam war. The cost of financing that war and the stimulus it provided to the US economy (since it was not offset by tight monetary or fiscal policy) took unemployment to low levels for some time and inflation accelerated. This inflation was then transmitted to other countries, initially via the fixed exchange rate system of the time.

A second factor was the run-up in world commodity prices, particularly during the 1970s. For a time in the early 1970s it was widely believed that this rise reflected a dwindling in world natural resources. It is clear now, however, with the prices of most commodities back to the level of the early 1970s in real terms, that this was not a long term trend but a cyclical move. After over 20 years of strong growth in the USA and Europe, commodity producing capacity had temporarily fallen behind. Once prices moved up in the 1970s more capacity was created and prices were eventually driven down again.

A third general factor was the bias towards faster economic growth in most countries. Faster growth means a more rapid rise in living standards which is politically popular. Because inflation took time to pick up and because people got used to it, with the help of floating interest rates and indexation, it took many years for policy to turn decisively against inflation. The key year was 1979, when Paul Volcker, Chairman of the US Federal Reserve, switched policy and raised interest rates sharply, Mrs. Thatcher was elected to power in the UK and the Exchange Rate Mechanism was set up in Europe.

Indicators of inflation

The most commonly quoted measure of inflation is the *consumer price index* but there are a host of others. The CPI (or retail price index, RPI, in the UK) is a basket of commodities weighted roughly according to an average family's budget. It is often distorted by sharp movements in food prices and energy prices and by movements in indirect taxation, e.g. valued added taxes or other taxes. Hence, for example, the US publishes its CPI both in full and excluding food and energy. Rising food and energy prices can of course add to inflation over the long term but, very often, sharp monthly rises are subsequently reversed. The CPI in some countries can be distorted by special factors such as changes in interest rates, for example in the UK and Switzerland.

A second keenly watched indicator is the index of *wholesale or producer prices*, which measures the price of a basket of goods at the wholesale level. Another indicator is the *GDP deflator*. This is the index used to translate the calculation of nominal GDP into real GDP and therefore represents the price of all goods produced domestically.

Another way to think of inflation is to treat it as the sum of three components, *wage growth* minus *productivity growth* plus *margin growth*. This requires some explanation. If wages are increasing at, for example, 5% and productivity growth is increasing at 2% then prices are likely to be increasing at 3%, if producers and retailers are not altering their margins. If they are trying to raise margins then price inflation is likely to be higher than 3% and vice versa.

Margins tend to rise during the economic upswing and contract during a slowdown or recession so that price inflation swings around more than wage inflation. Nevertheless, while margins do impact on recorded price inflation it is the trend of wages which has more long run importance. The best measure of wages is *hourly earnings*, or, after taking productivity growth into account, *unit labour costs*.

Measuring The Forces on Inflation

The output gap

Economists look at two basic ideas in trying to measure whether the economy is positioned in such a way as to raise inflation or reduce inflation. These are called the output gap and the natural or non-accelerating rate of unemployment.

The output gap is a measure of the extent to which the economy is running above or below its trend rate of growth, i.e. whether there is a gap between what the output of the economy actually is and what it could be. If output has risen well above its trend line then the economy is likely to be overheating and vice-versa.

The chart overleaf shows an estimate of output versus trend for the US economy since 1960. It shows clearly that inflation tends to fall when an output gap emerges, for example in 1970-71, 1974-6, 1981-5, and 1990-3. Similarly inflation rises about one year after output goes above trend. Sometimes it is obvious whether the economy is well short of capacity or if it is showing signs of severe overheating. At other times it is a more questionable measurement. The output gap opens up when the actual output of the economy drops below estimates of the trend or the underlying growth rate of the economy. If the trend growth of the economy is thought to be 2.5% p.a. then economic growth at 4% for 2 or 3 years is likely to take the economy above its trend growth path, unless it begins after an especially deep recession.

USA: Output Gap and Inflation

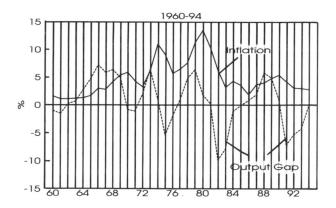

The natural rate of unemployment

Another way of measuring the forces on inflation is to look at the natural rate or unemployment (or the non-accelerating inflation rate of unemployment or NAIRU for short). This is the level of unemployment which is neither so low that wages are likely to move up or so high that wage settlements are likely to be trending down. As its name suggests, the non-accelerating inflation rate of unemployment is a rate which is neutral for inflation, neither boosting it or restraining it. The NAIRU used to be called the natural rate because some economists argued that the economy would naturally return to this level if left to itself, although this is a matter of debate.

Inevitably there are substantial disagreements on the level of the NAIRU in each economy. It is generally accepted as having risen over the last 20 years for a number of reasons discussed below but there is uncertainty over how much. Note that for the markets a key factor is what level of unemployment the monetary authorities regard as natural, or at least a range where they start to become concerned. For example, the Federal Reserve is believed to regard 6% as a level below which wage pressures are likely to increase and therefore usually begins tightening once unemployment approaches that level.

USA: Unemployment Gap and Inflation

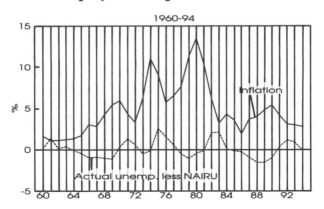

These concepts are important because they explain why, just because economies pick up and start to grow, inflationary pressures will not necessarily re-emerge straight away. After a long recession like the early 1990s, the output gap is well above what would be regarded as natural rates. Hence these economies can grow at relatively rapid rates, above trend growth rates, for at least a few years before inflation re-emerges. At the same time, a combination of recovery with low or declining inflation does not mean that inflation has gone away permanently, only that it is at bay.

Why is the NAIRU not zero?

A second question almost as often asked is, why has the natural rate of unemployment risen in the last 30 years? The best way to approach these questions is to look at the reasons for unemployment.

Firstly, there are people who have lost their job and take a little while to find a new job. For various reasons people spend longer finding a new job now than before (even when the economy is buoyant). This may be because they have more of a financial cushion and therefore can look around for a little longer rather than accepting the first job that comes their way. Or perhaps as jobs become more and more specialised it takes a little longer to find the right job. If on average people spend two months in between jobs now, whereas they spent only one month between jobs in the 1970s, then recorded unemployment will rise even though this may not represent an increase in slack in the economy.

Unemployment Rates 1961-89

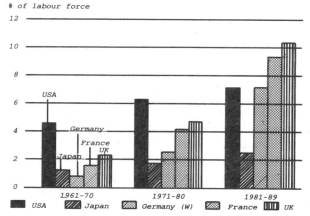

Secondly, there is structural unemployment, although this word "structural" covers a multitude of factors. Generally it means that people have the wrong skills or are in the wrong place to find jobs. For various reasons, including lack of adequate incentives or problems with relocating because of inefficiencies in housing markets (e.g. people cannot find cheap rented accommodation in the big city where the jobs are), people either do not learn new skills or remain in areas of high unemployment. As the pace of structural change in the world economy accelerates this problem has become more intense.

The *third* reason for unemployment is inadequate incentives to take work. If by taking work people lose too many benefits and face too much taxation, then the incentives to work are not great. In many countries, particularly in Europe, it would appear that there has been an increase in the number of people who register as unemployed and receive benefits but also do casual work in the "black economy". These people may be disinclined to return to normal taxed work because they would be worse off.

The first three causes of unemployment determine the NAIRU or natural rate. The final cause of unemployment is lack of "demand" owing to the state of the business cycle. It is this which takes the economy above or below the NAIRU rate and which we are trying to measure.

Inflation and Investors

Low inflation in the 1990s

After 20 years of relatively high inflation the prospect in the second half of the 1990s is for much lower inflation. In most of the industrial countries, inflation has converged to levels of 3% or below. Economists usually argue that low inflation is good news for growth although this point is hard to prove. Certainly there are plenty of examples of countries with high growth and high inflation, for example Japan before 1973 or Italy for much of the 1970s and 1980s.

Still, the theoretical arguments that low inflation produces higher growth are compelling. *Firstly*, lower inflation means that there is a more stable environment for company planning. High inflation tends to bring uncertainty over future prices for both inputs and outputs including foreign exchange, wages, interest rates, etc. While management can hedge against some of these uncertainties, it can usually do so only for the short term and some of them it cannot control at all. Investment therefore becomes a less risky business in a period of low inflation.

Secondly, with low inflation, the financial environment is more stable which allows real interest rates (the difference between nominal rates and inflation) to come down. This is because the danger of a sudden sharp acceleration in inflation is reduced and so investors require less of a risk premium. Lower rates of interest encourage more investment, boosting economic growth.

USA: Consumer Price Inflation

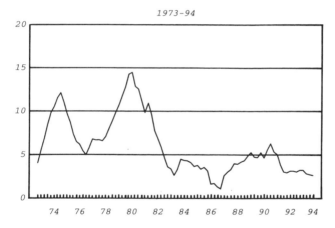

1973–94

Thirdly, low inflation can improve business cash flow. In periods of high inflation and high interest rates the cost of borrowing effectively becomes front-loaded because interest payments are high right from the beginning, while the repayment at the end of the term of the loan is in devalued money. Any investment financed by borrowing will therefore generate a less positive cash flow in the first few years in an environment of high inflation.

Fourthly, low inflation promotes growth by making changes in relative prices much more transparent both to consumers and businesses. When the general price level is moving upwards and price lists are frequently revised, it is harder for people to ensure they are paying or asking the right price. Since the market system relies for its efficiency on price signals, it is important that inflation does not obscure them.

Hence a low inflation environment is good news for economic growth and therefore good news also for investment returns measured in real terms. The problem though, is that the transition from high inflation inevitably includes a period of slow growth, high unemployment and reduced profits.

Inflation and investment returns

The general level of inflation has had a crucial influence on investment returns in the last three decades. The investor who judged that inflation was going to be high in the 1970s could have done well but the best investments were stocks and, for a period in the middle 1980s, property, while in the 1990s bonds and stocks thus far have offered the best returns. Between 1987 and 1991 in many countries cash deposits offered one of the best returns. Having an investment portfolio weighted towards the best-performing asset classes is the best way to make good long run returns and the key factor here is the rate of inflation.

The surge in inflation in the 1970s severely hurt the bond markets while the fall in inflation in the first part of the 1990s allowed bond markets to rally strongly. Property benefited in the 1970s particularly from inflation and in the 1980s partly from inflation and partly from other factors such as liberalisation of lending and the boom in demand for office space. Stock markets suffered in the 1974-5 recession and then held their own through the rest of the 1970s before growing very strongly in the 1980s when inflation came down.

In the low inflation environment of the early 1990s, property remained weak and although there has been a recovery in some sectors and some countries in 1994-5 it is unlikely to show substantial returns while inflation remains low. Industrial commodities, especially metals picked up sharply in 1994, in response to strong US growth but low general inflation is likely to continue to hold them back in comparison to the 1970s.

In the bond markets the problem is how to judge how low inflation will go and whether bond yields have fully adjusted. Many investors therefore argue that stocks offer the best long term return (which has indeed been the case over the very long run anyway) as the world economy goes through a prolonged upswing with contained inflation.

Nevertheless the key for successful long-term investing is to have a mixed portfolio including both stocks and bonds and probably property too. Having only bonds would be risky if inflation accelerates from here.

One of the problems facing investors in the 1990s is that low inflation means that nominal returns are comparatively lower even though real returns are as high or higher than before. In the 1970s or 1980s it was common for investments to return over 10% p.a. for years in succession. But US inflation averaged 5.8% between 1967-90. If inflation averages only 3% in the 1990s, returns would naturally be less. This may lead investors to seek higher risk investments even the reality is that they do not necessarily need to do so. In the end it is the real return, after inflation, which matters for investors.

4. Money and Interest Rates

Overview

The Operation of Monetary Policy

Monetarism: An Alternative Approach

Monetary Policy and the Exchange Rate

Overview

Monetary policy is the most closely watched indicator of economic policy mainly because governments alter their monetary policy stance much more frequently than fiscal policy. For the investor, understanding the aims of the monetary authorities and forecasting the next move is the single most important factor in analysing the markets.

The main instrument of monetary policy is the short term rate of interest. The exact interest rate instrument varies from country to country but it is usually an overnight rate or a very short term interest rate which the Central Bank can directly control. This short term rate of interest influences the rest of the yield curve, with a declining impact as it goes out in time.

At the far end of the yield spectrum, 30 year bond yields are only indirectly affected by overnight rates and indeed, in response to a move in money rates, can move in the same direction or the opposite direction or not at all.

A cut in short term interest rates will stimulate the economy and vice-versa though the size of the impact also depends on the level of interest rates relative to inflation, i.e. the "real" interest rate and a host of other factors. A cut in interest rates will also usually lower the exchange rate.

One group of economists, monetarists, believes that changes in the money supply are a better indicator of the stance of monetary policy than either interest rates or trends in the economy itself. But most economists and governments now distrust pure monetarism and only look at money growth alongside all the other indicators.

What are central banks trying to do?

In day-to-day markets changes in monetary policy or expectations of change dominate market activity. For the longer term investor monetary policy is important for being one of the key determinants of the business cycle. Governments cannot make recessions and recoveries to order, but they certainly try, and monetary policy is their main instrument. In the early 1990s the question was what rate of interest would get the economy growing fast enough to bring unemployment down. In the mid-1990s interest rates have been raised in many countries to slow growth.

The key variables that the monetary authorities watch are the pace of economic growth, the amount of excess capacity still available if any, (the "output gap", see chapter 3) and the rate of inflation.

Federal Reserve policy in the late 1980s

The approach of the US Federal Reserve in the late 1980s is revealing. At that time the Fed was trying to engineer a "soft landing" for the economy to deal with the acceleration in inflation from 2-3% in 1986 to around 4% in 1988. But controlling the economy like this is very difficult to achieve in practice as the outcome once again proved.

A useful analogy is to think of being in a pilot's seat trying to control an aircraft, i.e. the economy, into land. The anxious passengers, the markets, try to guess what the next move would be. A touch more on the airbrakes is used to slow the plane (e.g. a rise in interest rates), or keep things steady (no change) because the plane is nicely on the glidepath. Pursuing the analogy, the key instruments to watch are the altimeter, i.e. where the economy is in relation to full capacity, and the rate of descent indicator which shows how quickly the economy is moving towards full capacity.

One of the problems is that neither the central bank nor the markets can look out of the front window of the plane, but only behind them, as data on the past movement of the economy become available. Another problem is that there is a delay between any action by the Fed on the controls and the plane responding.

The Fed raised rates from 6% in 1987 to 10%

briefly in early 1989 and then cut them to 8¼% in the first half of 1990. Despite bringing rates down from the peak, history records that the Fed crashed! The economy went into recession in July 1990, one month before the Iraqi invasion of Kuwait.

In the early 1990s most of the major Central Banks went through the same attempted landing as the Fed and they all had crashed by 1992, though a cynic might say that this was what was intended. They were all trying to get inflation down (apart from some European countries like France which were just interested in retaining their exchange rate parities in the European Exchange Rate Mechanism) and the important thing was to get to ground level. A hard landing was better than an overshoot.

But that introduces another element into the analogy above. As well as the pilot and the markets there is also the "owner" of the plane, the government, which in most countries plays a role. Governments are interested in making sure that the plane is flying high when elections loom and they certainly do not want a crash landing.

In Europe the Exchange Rate Mechanism means that governments cannot operate an independent monetary policy even if they would like to. The ERM requires formation flying! In Germany and to a lesser extent the United States, the central banks have the government firmly strapped in a back seat. However fiscal policy can have a major effect on the plane and both the Fed and Bundesbank have been struggling to deal with the consequences of high budget deficits!

The Operation of Monetary Policy

Interest rates

The primary instrument of monetary policy is the short term interest rate. The monetary authorities alternately squeeze or flood banks' balance sheets with money in order to raise or lower short term interest rates to their target level. In the United States the key rate is the Federal Funds Rate, while in some other countries it is an overnight money rate or a repurchase rate. In the UK the banks' base rate is the key rate. These overnight or very short term rates in turn influence the whole of the yield curve. Many countries including the USA, Japan and Germany have a discount rate which is a rate at which banks can borrow from the central bank. This is usually below prevailing money rates and is available to banks only in exceptional cases.

Key official interest rates to watch

USA   *Federal Funds Rate* - the Federal Reserve's key rate. It is an overnight deposit rate for banks

   Discount Rate - always under Fed Funds rate. A change may signal an imminent move in Fed Funds rate and can sometimes affect Bank's prime rate, independently of the Fed Funds rate

Japan *Official discount rate* - the floor for rates

Germany
   Repurchase rate - the key operating interest rate
   Lombard rate - the ceiling for short-term market rates
   Discount rate - the floor for short-term markets rates

UK   Bank of England's *dealing rates*. Used to control bank's *base rates*

The yield curve

The yield curve is a chart of interest rates from overnight rates out to 30 year bond yields, or even beyond, at any particular moment in time. To use a different flying analogy from the one above, the yield curve can be seen as a kite string with the monetary authorities hanging on to the end. The lower part of the string is not going to be far up or down from where the central bank is holding it, but at the other end of the string, at longer maturities, the kite could be very steeply up in the air or sloping down to the ground. If the markets think that the government might lower its short term rate soon then 3 month interest rates might even be below overnight rates. While if the government does tug on the string and reduce interest rates the effect might be, as kite-flying enthusiasts know, to take the kite higher with a steeper angle on the string (yield curve).

USA: Money and Bond Yields

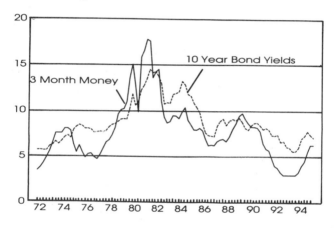

A "normal" yield curve has an upward slope (i.e. bond yields above money-rates) because, for investors to lend for a longer period, requires a higher return to justify the risk. If investors think that government controlled interest rates are headed up then the yield curve will be especially steep. If however investors think that the government may be going to cut interest rates then long term rates may be below short term rates, i.e. the yield curve is "inverted". Usually, at the height of an economic upswing the yield curve is inverted while, at the end of a recession and beginning of a recovery, the curve will be normal and indeed steeply upward-sloping. As the chart overleaf shows, the yield curve is a good leading indicator of the economy.

Interest rates and the economy

A cut in interest rates will normally stimulate the economy and vice-versa, though the precise impact is always uncertain. The change in short term interest rates affects the economy through a number of different mechanisms which vary in their effects at different times. The best way to look at this is in terms of the components of GDP (consumer spending, business spending, government spending and foreigners' spending).

US Yield Curve and the Cycle

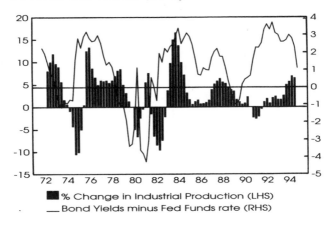

■ % Change in Industrial Production (LHS)
__ Bond Yields minus Fed Funds rate (RHS)

Consumers tend to spend more when interest rates are lower for various reasons. *Firstly*, lower rates encourage more borrowing particularly for the big-ticket items such as cars and kitchens. In the UK, where most housing finance is at floating interest rates, consumers benefit very quickly from lower mortgage payments. In other countries where fixed rate mortgage finance is more common, lower interest rates may have some negative impact on consumers by reducing interest income. *Secondly*, lower interest rates usually bring a fall in yields across the spectrum which means higher bond and stock prices. This in turn should encourage consumers to go out and spend.

Business will be more inclined to spend too for similar reasons. Investment projects are more attractive if they can be financed at lower interest rates. Lower interest rates often mean higher share prices which encourage businesses to invest. Small businesses in particular are often very much influenced by interest rates. In the short run, however, interest rates probably influence business spending more through being signals about the direction of the economy (e.g. lower interest rates point to faster growth ahead) which encourages retailers to order more goods and companies to produce more in anticipation. Lower interest rates also help by improving business balance sheets, to the extent that they use floating rate debt. Interest rates work on foreigners' spending by influencing the exchange rate. Usually a cut in rates will lower the exchange rate and therefore stimulate exports.

Assessing the policy stance

The extent to which a particular move in short term interest rates will stimulate the economy is always difficult to judge in advance. We do know that the full effect is not complete for a year or more. Although confidence may receive an immediate boost from lower interest rates, the impact on spending takes longer.

The effect of a cut in rates also depends on the absolute level of interest rates, not just the direction of change. For example, if interest rates have been raised from 6 to 10% to deal with inflation and then in response to a recession are lowered to 7%, the lowering of interest rates might stimulate the economy, but interest rates are still at higher levels than where they started.

Economists often look at *real* interest rates, i.e. the difference between interest rates and inflation, to judge how easy or tight policy is at that moment. In the above example, if inflation is running at 4% and interest rates are at 7% the real interest rate would still be 3%, which would normally be judged comparatively high to stimulate spending. Ideally the calculation of the real interest rate should use *expectations* for inflation rather than just the latest figure. If the economy is weak then the chances are that inflation is headed down, i.e. inflation expectations are lower than actual inflation and the implied real interest rate is correspondingly higher.

The trouble with using real interest rates as a guide is that they have varied at different points in history. The whole of the 1980s economic upswing took place with comparatively high real interest rates, whereas in the 1970s real interest rates were mostly negative. In the 1990s real interest rates have been low so far for the United States. One reason is that fiscal policy is not stimulatory in contrast to the early 1980s. Another is that the problems of weak balance sheets and excessive debt burdens have made everybody more cautious about using debt. Finally the problems of many banks meant that there was a wider than usual gap between money rates and actual lending rates in the early 1990s.

USA: Real Interest Rates

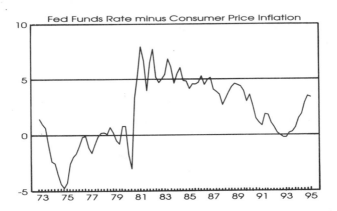

Fed Funds Rate minus Consumer Price Inflation

Monetarism: An Alternative Approach

The difficulty with using real interest rates as an indicator of policy stance is one reason why many monetarist economists believe that changes in money supply are a better indicator of the position of monetary policy. Another reason is that monetarists believe that changes in money supply occur *before* changes in the real economy and therefore can be used as a leading indicator of the economy.

Most monetarists would disagree little with the paragraphs above describing the relationship between changes in interest rates and the economy. However they would regard the interest rate story as being only a "transmission mechanism" between the money supply and the real economy. For example a rise in the money supply causes a fall in interest rates which causes the economy to strengthen.

However, monetarists split into two groups on this point, with some believing that changes in the money supply *cause* changes in the real economy and in prices, while others believe that money supply is just a particularly good indicator. It is thought to indicate movements in the economy with a lead time of between 3 months and 2 years.

The great age of monetarism 1976-85

Monetarism is not new and in fact goes back to early in this century and before. It has long been known that, over the long term, a relationship exists between the money supply and the economy. Even Keynes himself, frequently accused of ignoring money, in fact wrote most of his major works on the subject of money. However his followers, the Keynesians, after the Second World War, accorded money very little importance. They argued that fiscal policy should be the main instrument of control over the economy. It was only when these policies seemed to fail that monetarism was re-discovered by main-stream economists and policy-makers.

During the 1970s inflation reached crisis levels and governments seemed unable to control it. There was a widespread rejection of Keynesian economics and macro-economic policy began to follow a monetarist approach. The great monetarist experiments in the US and the UK around the end of the 1970s and in the early 1980s were founded on the belief that controlling the money supply was the key to controlling inflation. Some even argued that it would be relatively painless, a claim now usually forgotten.

Once governments tried directly to control money supply, under Mrs Thatcher in 1979-85 and under Paul Volcker at the Federal Reserve, during 1979-82, the result was a massive rise in interest rates. This was not very surprising, but what did surprise everybody was a massive rise in money supply, at least at first. This was partly due to the rise in interest rates itself which encouraged people to hold wealth in interest bearing securities, included in broad money measures, rather than stocks or bonds which are not.

Eventually inflation did come down substantially but only through the usual mechanism of a severe recession and high unemployment. Meanwhile money growth was high and volatile and the historical link between money and inflation seemed to have broken down. By the mid 1980s both the US and the UK authorities had rejected the idea that money could be relied upon as the sole or even the main guide to policy.

Some people now regard that as a mistake. For example, in the UK, rapid money growth in the 1980s did signal the excessive boom of the late 1980s, the rise in asset prices and the acceleration in inflation. Other indicators showed that too, including asset prices themselves, the dramatic fall in unemployment and the pace of growth of the economy itself, but unfortunately none of the indicators were heeded until it was too late. Nevertheless the authorities are now swinging back to giving more role for money but only in the context of other indicators.

Most governments still set monetary targets but now, if money goes outside these targets, governments will not necessarily respond nor will the markets immediately draw conclusions. The major exception here is the Bundesbank which still relies on money supply data as an indicator. Even in Germany, however, the distortions in the money supply caused by unification and other factors in recent years have sometimes forced the Bundesbank to discount the money supply.

Which money measure?

A key problem for monetarism and a major topic of debate among monetarist economists is which measure of money supply to use. Ideally the measure would include only money which people hold ready for spending, e.g. cash and chequing accounts. But experience has suggested that other forms of money including short-term deposits may also be held for spending soon so most monetarists prefer to look at wider measures. However the wider the measure the more likely that some of the accounts may not be intended for short term spending.

Money: US Definitions

Notes and coin

+ Travellers cheques
+ demand/sight deposits   = M1

+ repurchase agreements
+ savings deposits under $100,000
+ money market funds   = M2

+ large time deposits
+ institution-only money market funds
+ certain overseas amounts help by Americans   =M3

See Federal Reserve Bulletin for complete listing

Money measures are listed from M0 to M4 with slight differences in definition between countries though the concepts are similar. The narrowest measure of money is called the monetary base and consists of just banks' reserves at the central bank and cash in circulation. This is known as M0 in the UK and is a closely watched indicator of the strength of the economy. Past evidence suggests that M0 is closely correlated with spending in the economy, though without more than a few weeks' lead time. Money supply M1 is M0 plus sight or demand deposits. M2 includes large time deposits, while M3 includes large time deposits and money market funds.

In times of higher interest rates, people may in fact hold more assets in higher interest accounts rather than chequing accounts. They may also hold fewer bonds or stocks. Economists have spent an enormous amount of time analysing the relationship between the level of interest rates and the form in which people hold their money. One of the biggest issues in the literature on monetarism is whether or not this relationship is stable. If it is stable then when we see a rise in the quantity of money we will know whether it is simply due to changed interest rates or whether it indicates faster economic growth.

The velocity of money

Velocity is the measure of the speed with which money goes round the economy. Each individual or company spends money or writes a cheque and passes it to somebody else who may keep that money in their account for a few weeks and then themselves write a cheque or draw out cash to spend. The amount of money measured at any one time in the economy, i.e. the stock of money, is going to be less than the sum of all transactions during the year (i.e. Gross Domestic Product plus all purchases of assets e.g. second-hand cars, stocks or property) because money is flowing around from person to person.

The key question for monetarism is whether the velocity of money is stable. It does not necessarily have to be constant. We know that it might be affected by changes in interest rates. We also know that there may be long term trends involved, for example as people increasingly use credit cards. But neither point matters if the authorities can make allowances for higher or lower rates or long term trends. We would know that a rise in money supply after allowing for short-term cyclical factors or long-run trends implied an increase in transactions.

However we would not automatically know whether an increase in the value of transactions represented an increase in prices or an increase in the number of transactions. Nor could we know whether it represented an increase in demand for current output (i.e. GDP) or an increase in transactions of assets, for example more house sales.

Velocity has been unstable

In practice velocity has changed over time and sometimes in an unpredictable way, which makes the relationship difficult to sustain. The stable relationship which appeared to exist in the 1960s and 1970s became less stable in the late 1970s and 1980s. It is believed that this could be due either to the financial innovations of the later period or it might have to do with the effects of targeting money supply. One of the key Bank of England officials involved in managing the UK's monetarist experiment, Charles Goodhart, coined "Goodhart's law" which stated that whichever monetary aggregate is chosen as a target variable becomes distorted by the very act of choosing it as a target!

The rapid growth of money supply in a number of countries in the mid 1980s was, initially at least, linked to the rapid turnover in assets such as property and shares. Only later in the decade did the economies become sufficiently heated for a general rise in prices. Whether the build-up of general inflation could have been avoided if governments had managed to slow the economy early enough is an unanswerable question. Governments were tightening policy sharply in 1987 but then reversed for 6 months or more after the October stock market crash.

The jury is still out on money as an indicator

Monetarist economists still believe that careful analysis of money data is revealing and indeed, if we accept Goodhart's law, this may be more true if governments are not using monetary targets. Non-monetarists have given up, or use money supply only alongside all the other data, partly because they doubt the usefulness of monetary developments as an indicator of economic developments and partly because they know that central banks are looking at everything else too.

Most governments still find that money developments are not very helpful in making short run policy and prefer to look out of the window, even the back window to see where they are, rather than rely on money numbers. For this reason the markets now pay far more attention to data releases on employment and production than they do to money supply. The longer term investor however should definitely not exclude monetary trends from his calculations.

Monetary Policy and the Exchange Rate

The basic rule is that a government cannot have an interest rate (or monetary) policy independently from an exchange rate policy. The reason is simple: if the government tries to maintain a particular exchange rate then interest rates may have to rise at times if people don't believe that the exchange rate is sustainable, or fall at other times to prevent the exchange rate rising.

Another rule, however, which became very clear in Europe in 1992-3, is that a pure exchange rate policy will not necessary work. In effect, although governments can and at times in the early 1990s did, raise short term rates to astronomically high levels (for example 1000% at an annualised rate overnight), if markets do not anticipate that this level can continue, the government is liable to be forced to devalue anyway.

However if the government is pursuing an exchange rate policy then interest rates are the easiest and quickest way to do it. A cut in interest rates will usually bring the exchange rate down, encouraging the economy. Similarly a rise in interest rates often slows the economy and reduces inflation, particularly through maintaining or raising the exchange rate. The mechanism here is that a high exchange rate puts pressure on domestic producers to control prices and that feeds through the whole economy.

5. Fiscal Policy

Overview

Measuring the Stance of Fiscal Policy

Structural balances
The UK experience

Why Fiscal Policy Does Not Always Work

A theoretical argument
Crowding out
"Temporary" policy

Linkages with Monetary Policy

Policy mix and the yield curve

Fiscal Policy in Practice

The US experience
German experience since unification
Real interest rates
Fiscal policy in high inflation countries
Fiscal policy and debt
Fiscal policy and politics

Conclusion: Fiscal Policies and Markets

Overview

Fiscal policy works through changes in the government budget deficit which alter the amount of spending in the economy and therefore influence sales and production. For example a cut in tax rates or a rise in government spending will both tend to stimulate the economy while a rise in tax rates or a cut in government spending constrain the economy. The main impact of fiscal policy in the markets is on bond markets with an expansionary policy tending to raise bond yields and a contractionary policy lowering bond yields. The responses of the currency and stock markets depend on the mix of fiscal and monetary policy.

Fiscal policy is one of the two main policy areas that governments use to manipulate and control the economy. The other is monetary policy, although in practice fiscal and monetary policy are often directly or indirectly linked. Generally speaking fiscal policy is a slower and more ponderous instrument than monetary policy, both more difficult for the government to change and slower to act on the economy. However, for countries following an exchange rate policy, e.g. the members of the Exchange Rate Mechanism in Europe for whom monetary policy is dependent on the Bundesbank, fiscal policy takes on a greater importance.

Note however that fiscal policy has a longer time lag than monetary policy. Whereas the impact of changes in monetary policy usually takes around 3 months to come through and is likely to be exhausted after 12 months, fiscal policy generally acts over a period between 9 months and two years.

In analysing fiscal policy, or the so-called "fiscal stance", it is crucial to remember two points. Firstly it is *changes* in the fiscal deficit which matter, not its level. For example although the Italian budget deficit has been running at 10% of GDP or more for many years this is not imparting a continuous stimulus to the economy. But if one year the deficit rises to 12% that could represent a stimulus. Secondly only those changes in the deficit which are due to *deliberate changes* in government policy matter. The budget deficit will constantly be changing in response to the economy. During recessions the deficit tends to rise because tax revenues fall and government spending on unemployment benefits increases. In contrast, when the economy grows strongly, the budget deficit naturally falls. However, if, in a given year, the deficit rises because of a reduction in tax rates or a rise in government spending, then there is a stimulus.

The tendency for the deficit to rise in recessions and fall in booms is an important source of stability for the economy, helping to avoid major downturns or depressions. The power of so-called "automatic stabilisers" has only really emerged since the Second World War as government spending has risen to 30-50% of GDP and therefore the amounts in relation to the economy mattered. Before the Second World War, government spending in most countries amounted to often only around 10-15% of GDP.

Measuring the Stance of Fiscal Policy

Structural balances

Some governments prefer to obscure the extent to which changes in the budget deficit are due to government action and the extent to which they are in response to the economy. But the OECD regularly publishes measures of the "structural balance" of the government finances, expressed as a percent of GDP. The structural balance calculates what the deficit would be if the economy was at its trend output level, i.e. neither in recession nor overheating.

Until recently, with most countries still recovering from recession and therefore still with large output gaps, government structural deficits have been significantly less than actual deficits *(see table overleaf)*. Japan went through the recession with a small financial deficit but still had a structural surplus. Note however that these data are not comprehensive where countries have significant off-budget items. For example, in Germany if the deficit of the Treuhand and national railways was included, the financial deficit would be over 5% of GDP.

Changes in the structural balance *(the last column in the table)* represent actual fiscal policy. A fall in the structural deficit or rise in the surplus (i.e. a positive change) is a tightening of policy and vice-versa. In the early 1990s many countries used fiscal stimulus to offset the recession, for example the US in 1991-2 and the UK and France in 1992-3. However in 1994 only Japan was using fiscal stimulus. The other major countries were all tightening to some degree and continued to tighten in 1995.

Fiscal Stance 1994

% of GDP	Financial Balance	Structural Balance	Change in Structural Balance* 1993-4
USA	-2.6	-2.9	+0.4
Japan	-1.9	0.8	-1.1
Germany	-2.9	-2.3	+0.8
France	-5.9	-2.5	+0.4
UK	-6.4	-4.3	+1.0
Italy	-9.7	-6.6	+0.3

Source: OECD

* + ve sign indicates tightening

The UK experience

The UK provides a fascinating example of how ordinary financial deficits and structural deficits are influenced by the economic cycle and fiscal policy. Remember the basic rule is that structural deficits are influenced only by policy while the financial deficit moves with both policy and the economy.

In 1978/9 the UK had a high deficit on both measures *(see chart)*. At that time the economy was growing quite fast and had moved above trend level, with unemployment down to 4.5% in 1979. Hence the financial deficit was less than the structural deficit. Between 1980 and 1982 both deficits were sharply reduced despite a severe recession. This was partly due to the fiscal austerity introduced by the incoming Conservative government led by Mrs Thatcher though was substantially due to the sharp rise in government revenues from North Sea oil. Of course, because of the recession, the structural deficit moved lower than the financial deficit.

UK: General Government Balance

Financial and Structural, % of GDP

— Financial   ····· Structural

Through most of the 1980s the structural deficit remained at around 2-3% of GDP, but as the economic boom took hold the financial balance improved relative to the structural balance and in 1988 moved into surplus. The government was reluctant to tighten, partly because of forecasts, wrong as they turned out, that the economy was about to slow down on its own, as well as signals such as the 1987 stock market crash. However this lesson has been noted and governments generally are likely to be much more willing to run large surpluses in the 1990s. New Zealand, one country well ahead in the current economic cycle, is already planning for a surplus.

During the recent recession the UK financial deficit naturally soared. But the structural deficit rose too in 1992-3 indicating an expansionary fiscal policy. This may be seen either as a rational response to the impotence of monetary policy (until September 1992 when Sterling left the ERM) or a calculated (and successful) bid for re-election by the Conservative government.

The chart also shows trends in 1994-5. The combination of large tax increases and tight spending curbs is bringing the structural deficit back to the 2-3% range in 1995. The financial deficit will still be higher reflecting the expectation of continuing slack in the economy.

Why Fiscal Policy Does Not Always Work

Many economists question the effectiveness of fiscal policy. A few believe it is totally ineffective while most believe that although it can have an effect in the short term, the impact may be uncertain and can be partially offset by other factors. There are three broad arguments put forward for why fiscal policy may not work.

A theoretical argument

Firstly there is an argument that tax payers are not easily fooled. They recognise that the government deficit will have to be paid for in the end through higher taxes even though it is temporarily financed by bond issues. According to this theory people will view a reduction in taxation or increase in government spending as an increase in their future tax liability and therefore will increase their savings in response to it, ready to pay higher taxes further down the road. While this is a neat theoretical argument it seems to presuppose that taxpayers look ten or twenty years into the future and regard events then as holding a high degree of certainty. In an uncertain world, both for individuals and for the economy, this theory (known as the Ricardian equivalence theory) seems highly implausible.

Crowding out

The *second* and much more realistic objection to fiscal policy is the "crowding out" thesis. According to this idea if the government increases its spending and finances it by issuing bonds then the effect will be a rise in bond yields which "crowds out" spending by businesses and households unwilling to pay higher interest rates. The stimulatory effect of the government deficit is therefore cancelled out.

Most economists and governments believe that crowding out is less likely under two conditions. Firstly, if the economy is in recession then private spending is likely to be weak and spare resources in the form of labour and equipment are easily available. Secondly, if this easier fiscal policy is accompanied by easy monetary policy then any tendency for interest rates to rise will be offset.

Much depends on timing. If the fiscal expansion kicks in late, when the economy is already picking up, then it can raise interest rates. This is always a risk given the long lead time in fiscal policy. Or, if the monetary authority is independent like the Bundesbank or the Federal Reserve, it may see it as its duty to raise interest rates to offset the fiscal stimulus. As the economy recovers, household savings typically come down as people start to believe that the worst of the recession is over and unemployment is becoming a dwindling threat. Similarly business is likely to be accumulating inventories, which means increased borrowing, and perhaps looking to new investment. Hence "crowding out" is a possibility if fiscal policy is implemented any time other than during a recession.

On the other hand there will be times when a relaxation in both fiscal and monetary policy will be of great concern to the bond markets because they will anticipate higher inflation down the road. If governments look too keen to stimulate the economy when perhaps it is not that weak or inflation is seen as too high then the bond markets may sell off substantially.

"Temporary" policy

The *third* problem with the use of fiscal policy is when governments try to use it as a temporary device. For example, a special income tax surcharge for one year, or perhaps an income tax cut to be financed by a rise in other taxes after a two year delay will impart a temporary budget deficit to the economy and therefore should stimulate spending. The problem is that if households or businesses know this is strictly temporary they may not react very much. Nevertheless it is hard to believe that even these approaches will not have some impact, particularly if supported by monetary policy. The question is only over how much impact.

Linkages with Monetary Policy

When looking at policy it is useful to consider the overall mix of fiscal and monetary policy. If both fiscal and monetary policy are tight, then the situation is unambiguous and the economy is certain to slow after the necessary lags. Similarly if both monetary and fiscal policy are expansionary, then the economy can be expected to expand. However very often the policy settings are at odds with one another, for example with tight fiscal policy and loose monetary policy or vice versa. These situations create opportunities for investors as well as risks.

Policy mix and the yield curve

The fiscal/monetary mix often shows up in the shape of the yield curve, i.e. the relative position of short term interest rates and long term bond yields. The diagram overleaf illustrates the four possibilities. When both fiscal and monetary policy are loose the yield curve tends to be steeply upward sloping, i.e. bond yields are substantially above short term rates. When fiscal policy is tightened while monetary policy remains loose bond yields tend to fall and the yield curve comes back to a more moderate upward slope.

If monetary and fiscal policy are both tight then the yield curve is typically inverted, i.e. short rates move above long bond yields. Finally, when monetary policy is tight but fiscal policy is loose the yield curve tends to be flat, i.e. not much difference between short term rates and long bond yields. These four possibilities are well illustrated in the following examples from US and German experience.

Policy Mix and Yield Curve Shape

		Fiscal Policy	
		Loose	Tight
Monetary Policy	Loose	Steep	Moderate
	Tight	Flat	Inverted

Fiscal Policy in Practice

The US experience

In the early and mid 1980s the so-called supply-side policies of President Reagan involved a major loosening of fiscal policy. The US structural budget deficit increased by 1.8% of GDP between 1981 and 1983. The effect was to stimulate the economy strongly. In response the Federal Reserve kept interest rates high with the Federal Funds rate remaining above 9% even though inflation came down to 3-4%.

In the markets bond yields also remained high, averaging 11% in 1983 despite low inflation. This was because of the combination of high bond issuance, strong private demand for capital, a rapidly growing economy and high short term interest rates. As a result the yield curve was comparatively flat in this period. The dollar soared in the early 1980s reaching a peak in February 1985, attracted by the high nominal and real interest rates available. The stock market also liked this policy despite the high interest rates since the growth in the economy generated a strong recovery in profits.

In the late 1980s monetary policy was tightened again while fiscal policy became neutral, taking short rates above long rates (an inverted yield curve). In 1991-2 as the economy slowly recovered from recession both fiscal and monetary policy were loosened leading to a steeply upward sloping yield curve. Then in 1993 President Clinton's new budget package tightened fiscal policy leading to a strong rally in bonds and a flattening of the curve. In early 1994 interest rates were raised but monetary policy was initially still seen as too loose. Bond yields rose by a similar amount keeping the yield curve still moderately steep. In early 1995 the yield curve flattened as the markets began to anticipate a slowdown in the economy, and believed the Fed had tightened enough.

German experience since unification

German unification encouraged the Federal government in 1990-91 to provide large transfers to eastern Germany while raising taxes on West Germany only moderately. The budget deficit expanded dramatically and the Bundesbank offset this stimulus by raising interest rates significantly. The yield curve became inverted in 1992.

As in the USA in the mid 1980s the currency was strong with the Deutschemark hitting peaks of DM1.38 to the dollar in 1992 and forcing the weaker members of the exchange rate mechanism to devalue or exit the system. In 1993, with fiscal policy switching back to contractionary, short term interest rates came down sharply bringing a flat yield curve. In 1994, with signs of an economic recovery, bond yields rose sharply and the yield curve returned to an upward slope.

Real interest rates

If fiscal policy is stimulatory it will tend to raise *real* interest rates (i.e. interest rates minus inflation) and if it is contractionary it will tend to lower real interest rates. The reason is the effect of "crowding out" as described above. When the government is borrowing in the markets it is competing with the private sector for funds. This drives up interest rates, particularly at the medium and long term end of the yield curve. The effect is to take bond yields higher than they might otherwise be and strengthen the currency. Similarly if fiscal policy is contractionary then real bond yields and therefore often nominal bond yields will be falling. At the same time the exchange rate will tend to be weak.

Of course if monetary policy is expansionary at the same time as fiscal policy then there is no reason for there to be any particular pressure on interest rates at the short end of the curve. Banks will be awash with liquidity and there is no real "crowding out". However, further up the curve bond markets may be concerned about the inflation implications which is why this combination tends to generate a steep upward sloped yield curve with an unusually large spread between short rates and long rates.

Fiscal policy in high inflation countries

For countries with low inflation there is little direct link between fiscal policy and the level of inflation. For example in 1988-9, when the UK ran a budget surplus, inflation was accelerating because the private sector was booming. However in countries with high inflation, 5-10% or more, there is usually a direct link between fiscal policy and inflation. Inflation is being generated by direct printing of money (i.e. central bank financing) to pay for the budget deficit.

Using money growth to finance a fiscal deficit is sometimes referred to as the "inflation tax". Instead of collecting a normal tax like income tax or sales tax the government allows (or forces) the central bank to buy its bonds which means that the central bank is pushing money into the economy. This money creates inflation and that represents a tax on anybody who holds bank deposits or cash. Even during high inflation most people have some deposits and cash since it is usually unavoidable. When those deposits are worth, for example, 10% less at the end of the month than at the beginning of the month, this effectively represents a tax which is being collected by the government issuing the currency.

Fiscal policy in high inflation countries becomes almost entirely a question of whether and when the government can control its basic fiscal position. Typically the problem is that it is difficult to raise ordinary taxes further because of resistance to paying taxes, through evasion and avoidance. In periods of high inflation it is often very difficult to collect tax at all because tax payers know that if they can delay paying, even for a month or two, the effective burden is reduced. Also typically these governments are unable, due to social and political pressures, to cut spending. Success in reducing inflation depends on solving the fiscal problem. Any number of new currencies, price freezes or currency pegs will not work without it.

Fiscal policy and debt

For countries which have borrowed substantially in the past, a large government debt will have developed. There is no particular level beyond which debt can be said to be excessive although it is sometimes argued that if the ratio of debt/GDP is below 60% (the level for example specified in the Maastricht Treaty) then this level is satisfactory and can be managed. When debt moves up to near the 100% level or above as for example in Italy, Canada and Belgium, then the effect is to severely constrain government policy. The scope for fiscal stimulus in a recession is minimal because of the effect on confidence and the dangers to the debt position.

In practice it becomes difficult to reduce the

budget deficit because of the large volume of interest payments. For example a government with a debt/GDP ratio of 100% facing interest rates of 7% will pay an interest payments bill of 7% of GDP. With government spending in most industrial countries in the 40-45% range this means that 15-20% of spending is on interest payments. Reductions in spending therefore have to focus on the other 80% unless interest rates can be brought down. For these countries then there will be a tendency for bond yields to be high because of the risk of default as well as because of the volume of issuance in the markets. The markets may also demand high bond yields for fear that the government will try to inflate out of the problem.

Reducing government debt/GDP ratios takes a very long time. It is unlikely that even a very stringent policy will reduce the ratio by more than about 5% of GDP per year. For a country starting with a ratio of over 100% it will therefore take a decade to reduce the ratio to an acceptable 50% level.

Public Debt/GDP 1994

%	Gross	Net
USA	64.6	39.9
Japan	78.7	8.0
Germany	53.2	38.8
France	56.0	32.0
Italy	123.2	121.7
UK	52.0	45.6
Canada	95.6	65.2

Source: OECD

Note: Net debt includes government financial assets including social security surpluses (notably large for Japan)

Fiscal policy and politics

Inevitably fiscal policy is very closely bound up with politics where the responsibility has been given to independent central banks, as in Germany, the

United States or France. However fiscal policy is very much in the hands of governments. To some extent they can be disciplined by the markets through being forced to pay higher bond yields or facing a currency crisis if they pursue imprudent policies, but there is little getting away from the political process, especially close to elections. Cynics usually anticipate that the best time for fiscal tightening will be shortly after elections and they are often proved right. Cynics also expect fiscal loosening coming up to elections and again in many countries that is sometimes the case.

Tax cuts are popular, spending increases are popular and balanced budgets or reduced budget deficits are also popular, a combination which is impossible to square. However in the United States the warnings of economists that the US budget deficit would lead to trouble does seem to have gradually permeated the population so that in the 1990s there is strong political support for dealing with the budget deficit despite the pain. The same may be true of Italy. However in Canada Prime Minister Mulroney lost the 1993 election partly because of continued fiscal and monetary austerity under his government.

Conclusion: Fiscal Policies and Markets

From the discussion above we can generalise as follows. A deliberately stimulatory fiscal policy (i.e. a rise in the structural deficit) will usually be bad for the country's bond market. The reason is partly that it implies more bond issuance (though that in itself does not always matter) but more importantly that it points to a stronger economy in 1-2 years and therefore higher inflation than would occur without the stimulus.

Quite often a stimulatory policy will also be good for the currency because of the effect of higher interest rates and bond yields. It will also often be good news for stocks because of the prospect of faster growth and higher profits. However, both stocks and the currency could go the other way if the stimulatory fiscal policy is seen as mistimed or reckless. It would be mistimed if it occurred any time other than in a recession, either because the economy recovered earlier than expected or if it was put in place to win an election by a spendthrift government. A stimulatory policy would be reckless if it occurred when the government's debt ratio was already worryingly high.

A tightening of fiscal policy is generally good for the bond markets. If it is offset by looser monetary policy it is even better. The currency is likely to fall in both cases because of lower interest rates. The stock market will usually respond well to tighter fiscal policy, particularly if it is accompanied by looser monetary policy, provided only that it does not appear over-severe, risking a recession. Stock markets will react particularly favourably if the tightening is part of a long term programme to reduce government debts. With debts having risen sharply for many countries over the last three years the markets will be looking for a continuing tightening of structural deficits in the rest of this decade.

6. Trade and the Balance of Payments

Key Concepts

Definitions
Main items in the balance of payments

What Causes Current Account Imbalances?

Key role of savings-investment balance
Twin deficits
How excess savings cause surpluses
The cycle of capital and trade flows
Temporary versus chronic imbalances
Financing of current account deficits
Sustainability of deficits

Trade Data and the Markets

When trade data are important
Trade and exchange rates
The J-Curve effect
Trade disputes and exchange rates

Why Economists Believe in Free Trade

Free trade versus protectionism
The politics of trade

Capital Flows

Trade and balance of payments issues affect investors in four ways. Firstly, trade data releases tell us something about the performance of the domestic economy, in particular whether exports and imports are doing well, both of which would suggest faster economic growth. Secondly, data releases on trade are at times important as an indicator of the direction of the exchange rate. This usually applies when the trade deficit is high and the markets are anxiously watching for an improvement. Whether or not a trade deficit really matters ultimately depends on whether it can be financed. If a devaluation is thought to be imminent then interest rates are likely to be higher and bond yields may rise. Thirdly, trade policy disputes can sometimes affect exchange rates, e.g. the ongoing dispute between Japan and the USA. Finally, capital flows, which must by definition offset any current account deficit on a net basis, are becoming larger and larger relative to trade flows and can have an important impact on exchange rate trends.

Key Concepts

Definitions

The trade balance is usually defined as the difference between exports and imports of goods although the US Commerce Department now includes data for services as well, which are growing fast. The *current account* of the balance of payments is the most useful overall indicator of trading flows. It includes trade in services and also income and payments on capital including interest and dividends, etc.

Any current account deficit has to be balanced by a surplus (a net inflow) on the capital account. Countries with current account surpluses, for example Japan, must see a net capital outflow. The capital account includes the balance of bank lending and borrowing, portfolio flows (e.g. purchases and sales of bonds and shares) and direct investment flows (direct investment in plant and machinery).

The current account balance is also equal to the difference between total domestic savings and total domestic investment which is known as the savings-investment balance. For example a country which is investing (in new machinery, buildings, houses, etc.) more than its total domestic savings can only do so with an inflow of foreign capital and this requires a current account deficit.

The *basic balance* includes the current account and long-term capital flows such as direct investment and portfolio flows. It is useful because it gives an indication of what may be the more stable flows, before the short term balancing items such as bank lending and changes in central bank reserves. The *overall balance* is the sum of the current and capital account before changes in reserves.

Main items in the balance of payments

Listing	Definition
CURRENT ACCOUNT	Key overall trade measure
Exports of goods	Sales of goods abroad
Imports of goods	Purchase of foreign goods
Trade Balance	Goods trade balance
Services: Credit	Sales of services, e.g. insurance, software, plus spending of foreign visitors
Services: Debit	Purchase of foreign services
Income: Credit	Dividends, interest, etc. received from abroad
Income: Debit	Payment of dividends, interest, etc.
Private Transfers	Net private payments, e.g. remittances from workers abroad
Official Transfers	Net official payments, e.g. overseas aid

continued ...

CAPITAL ACCOUNT

Direct Investment	Net direct investment in plant and machinery, etc.
Portfolio Investment	Net purchases/sales of shares, bonds, etc.
Other Capital	Sum of other items:
Resident Official Sector	Official borrowing or lending
Deposit Money Banks	Net change in bank lending
Net Errors and Omissions	Often very large
Overall Balance	Sum of all above items
Change in Reserves	Must equal previous line

What Causes Current Account Imbalances?

Key role of savings-investment balance

The key factor in determining current account deficits or surpluses is whether, in the economy overall, individuals, businesses and the government are saving more than they are borrowing, or vice-versa.

Savings are defined as the difference between incomes and *current* expenditure, as opposed to capital expenditure. Incomes include both individual and company incomes and government tax revenues. Current expenditure includes spending on anything which is used up straight-away, which is taken to be all household spending on goods and services (even though many items like cars and refrigerators last a long time). For businesses it includes spending on wages and salaries, telephone bills, etc. but not computers or other machinery. Governments nearly always spend more than they receive in tax revenues and therefore their net savings position is negative.

When an individual or business spends less than his/its income on current expenditure and uses the difference either to increase bank deposits or to buy stocks or bonds this is defined as saving, in economics. When a company buys equipment or builds a house for sale or rent it is investing. If total investment spending is greater than savings in the economy, then the need for finance causes pressure in the credit markets, interest rates are kept higher and money will flow in from abroad. The inflow of money causes the exchange rate to appreciate. After a little time exports slow and imports rise, soon bringing a current account deficit and a matching capital inflow.

Twin deficits

Countries with large current account deficits often have large government budget deficits. This is directly linked to the savings-investment balance. The balance of government savings plus private sector savings equal the current account balance. A government budget deficit means that the government is spending more than its income from taxation and must borrow the difference. Economists call this "dissaving" or negative savings. If the private sector is a net saver then the current account need not be in deficit, but if the private sector is merely in balance, or in deficit, then the current account will be in deficit.

How excess savings cause surpluses

If savings are higher than investment (as is usual in Japan) then the economy has funds to spare, interest rates will tend to be low in real terms (i.e. after inflation) and investors domestically will look to overseas markets for a higher yield. The outflow of funds will cause the exchange rate to fall which will, in time, bring higher exports and lower imports. The country will move into a position of current account surplus with a matching capital account deficit as the excess savings flow abroad.

The importance of this theory is ignored or conveniently forgotten by many people in the trade debate. It means that the solution to Japan's trade surplus is not simply to try to raise the yen by talking it up because, unless the saving-investment balance changes as well, the surplus will continue.

Nor will removing protectionist barriers necessarily reduce the trade surplus. For example, if Japan were suddenly to open up its markets, imports would certainly rise. But unless the savings-investment balance changed too, exports would rise as well to offset the rise in imports. The most likely way for this to happen would be for the exchange rate to fall. A paradox is therefore that the US companies who urge an opening up to more imports might be shocked to discover that the relative competitiveness of Japan actually improves as a result. Some US companies who may currently face real blocks to their exports would benefit but others would suffer.

The cycle of capital and trade flows

Since capital flows can change faster than trade can adjust, countries often move through a cycle of exchange rate over- or under-valuation, gradually changing trade and eventual exchange rate correction.

The United States provided a very good example of this in the 1980s. When Ronald Reagan became President he quickly moved to cut taxation and increase defence spending which resulted by 1982 in a large budget deficit. Since he also cut taxes on business investment and at the same time the Federal Reserve brought interest rates down, the US economy took off from the 1981-2 recession at a very smart pace. Interest rates rose because savings fell short of investment, resulting in heavy pressure on funds and encouraging an inflow of capital.

But capital can only flow into a country (on a net basis) to the extent of its current account deficit. The first effect therefore was to send the dollar surging to high levels. By 1985-86 the high dollar had hurt exports and encouraged imports so that the current account deficit had widened considerably and the matching net inflow of capital was almost identical to the budget deficit. Interest rates domestically therefore began to come down and this process was encouraged at the time by the Federal Reserve and the US government as well as foreign governments. It took several more years however for the resulting fall in the exchange rate to improve the trade position. By then the economy had slowed, domestic demand for funds had decreased and the economy was finally back into equilibrium from the shock that President Reagan had imposed.

Temporary versus chronic imbalances

A temporary rise in the trade deficit is often due simply to faster economic growth in that country than elsewhere. Faster growth sucks in imports and, with growth elsewhere slower, exports are likely to do less well. If the country with faster growth is reaching capacity constraints it may even be that goods destined for the foreign market are diverted to home markets where margins may be higher. When this is the primary reason for a trade deficit, policymakers and the markets are likely to be relatively relaxed about the exchange rate and regard the correction of the deficit as likely to be achieved through either slower growth at home or faster growth elsewhere.

Some countries show a long-run tendency to investment higher than savings or vice-versa. For example the USA, UK (pre and post the initial impact of North Sea oil), Australia and Canada all tend to run current account deficits over the long term. Japan and Germany (pre-unification) tend to run surpluses. There is usually no market pressure for surpluses to come down. However deficits may be unsustainable if they cannot be financed.

Financing of current account deficits

Often the crucial question of how long a deficit can continue depends on how easy it is to finance that deficit. If the economy is growing rapidly with strong investment and high levels of confidence, then interest rates are likely to remain high for some time and inflows of capital will continue. If however the trade deficit is being financed with high interest rates which look unsustainable because the economy is weak, then the situation is likely to last only a limited time. This was clearly the situation of some of the European Exchange Rate Mechanism countries in 1992/3 and also of Australia and Canada just emerging from recession in 1991-2.

Sometimes the way in which the trade deficit is being financed is informative. If it is through direct and portfolio investment then that may be a signal that the deficit is part of a high investment path for the economy and that the situation will be sustainable. But if the money is coming in to bank deposits, enjoying high interest rates, then the situation may be less sustainable.

Sustainability of deficits

Another key factor in financing current account deficits is whether the markets see the level and growth of foreign debt as sustainable. For example, Australia has had a trade deficit throughout its history and in itself this has not become a problem. The doubts have arisen when the deficit has become too large and the level of foreign debt has risen to high levels.

If foreign debt is rising at say 5% per year but the economy is growing at 5% or more (in nominal terms) then the ratio of foreign debt to GDP is not deteriorating and the situation may be stable in the long term. If however foreign debt is increasing at 5% per year and the economy only expanding at 2% then the situation will not be sustainable in the long run. The latter is more likely to be true if in fact the overspending by the population is mainly traced to higher levels of consumption.

For example in the United States during the 1980s deficits were not associated with higher levels of investment. This still need not necessarily mean that there is a problem but it does mean that the country is borrowing for present consumption rather than to increase the rate of growth of the economy.

Trade Data and the Markets

When trade data are important

The components of the trade balance, exports and imports, often tell us something about GDP growth in the economy. If both exports and imports are strong the country is doing well in overseas markets but also is growing fast and is therefore sucking in imports. If exports are doing well but imports not then the message is ambiguous.

Very often and, especially if an economy is reasonably close to being in balance on trade, this is all that investors are concerned about when looking at trade data. However at certain times and particularly when trade balances are a long way from zero, the releases may be taken by the markets as important for the direction of exchange rates. Sometimes the link is directly through policy while other times the markets believe that, with or without government backing, the exchange rate will move.

For example during the middle 1980s the US trade deficit was the most important monthly data release, much more significant for the markets than the monthly employment data which have taken over this role in recent years. The reason was that the US trade deficit was widely regarded as unsustainable. When the government-orchestrated decline in the dollar between February 1985 and 1987 did not immediately improve the trade deficit, the markets anticipated that, either through further government action or through the natural forces of supply and demand, the dollar would need to go lower still.

Trade and exchange rates

In a free floating system the exchange rate is set by the net savings-investment balance in the economy.

For example, Japan, with its chronic tendency to save more than it invests has a tendency towards an under-valued exchange rate normally. In contrast the UK and US, with lower savings than investment, usually have an over-valued rate.

Of course these are not completely static. During the late 1980s Japan enjoyed an investment boom which took investment up to near the level of savings. In consequence the exchange rate strengthened, as less capital flowed out, bringing a reduced current account surplus. After the economy went into recession in 1991, investment dropped sharply and the current account surplus rose in direct consequence. Although Japanese investors have shown some reluctance to invest long term overseas the money still flows out, either through the banking system or through foreign issues of yen bonds.

With fixed exchange rates, e.g. within the European Exchange Rate Mechanism, the savings-investment balance still controls the current account of the balance of payments. But instead of working through the (nominal) exchange rate it works through changing costs. A devaluation or fall in the currency comes to the same thing as a decline in wages (relative to another country), except that changes in wage levels take longer. If the required changes do not look like happening fast enough then the exchange rate link may well break.

The J-Curve effect

The effect of a devaluation will eventually be to improve the balance of trade. But the initial effect may be to worsen the trade position because prices change before volumes adjust. This is known as the J-curve effect and it may take 1 or 2 years before the trade deficit moves back in the right direction.

Take the UK as an example with its current trade of £120 bn in exports and £134 bn in imports, with a trade deficit of £14 bn. If Sterling is devalued by 10% against all currencies the immediate effect may be to raise the trade deficit. Exports will initially stay at the same level because volumes do not immediately change and companies do not immediately raise prices. Meanwhile, since the majority of imports arc invoiced in dollars, the value of imports in Sterling terms immediately rises. Hence the trade deficit worsens, the first part of a letter "J". With time British producers will be able either to raise prices (in Sterling terms) or increase volumes or both, while the volume of imports will fall because British buyers switch to domestic products. The trade balance will improve, the long side of the letter "J", and after a period of time, usually at least a year, the trade balance will be stronger than before the devaluation.

Trade disputes and exchange rates

The phenomenon of a large trade deficit knocking a currency down is a very common one, particularly in the English-speaking countries, such as Australia and the UK. However the reverse case has been seen in Japan in recent years. Large and rising trade surpluses in Japan encouraged the view that the yen would need to rise to bring those surpluses down. In part this was a response to statements by US government officials. The markets believed that the US government was so concerned to see the Japanese trade surplus fall, that it required either big changes in Japanese trade policy to achieve this or a large rise in the exchange rate. Hence news of high monthly surpluses or signs that the Japanese government was dragging its feet over changes in trade policy induced a capital inflow which took the yen higher.

Why Economists Believe in Free Trade

Free trade versus protectionism

Most economists are passionate believers in free trade as the ideal policy. There are two general lines of argument behind this belief. The *first* is a theoretical one, known as the theory of comparative advantage, first fully argued by David Ricardo in the mid 19th century. This theory does not just say that a country can gain by concentrating on producing whatever it is better at producing than another country. It is more subtle and much richer than this argument, (which incidentally would be called the "Theory of Absolute Advantage"). What comparative advantage means is that a country should concentrate on producing goods which it can produce *comparatively* well even if it is less efficient at everything than another country. The exchange rate will take care of competitiveness.

For example, the United States can probably produce both aircraft and shoes using less labour and raw materials than can India. That does not mean that India should not produce either of those, only that it should produce the one at which it is relatively better at, compared to the United States. The exchange rate makes sure that an hour of labour in India costs much less in the USA and so India finds itself competitive at exporting shoes.

In the modern world, it is often argued that the relevance of this theory is limited and there have been many attempts to discredit it, particularly in the last 10-15 years. It has been shown theoretically that a government might be able to use protectionist policies to improve its country's living standards under certain conditions. But it would still be better for the government to use other policies, such as subsidies, rather than protectionism. Moreover the backing for free trade is still firm among nearly all economists because of the second line of argument.

The *second* argument is that it is much better to leave trade, and indeed the economy generally, to free markets. Economists believe that, although it can be argued in theory that governments could intervene to protect particularly important industries or to help particular companies, in practice once trade policy becomes a political issue (as unfortunately it already has in most countries) the decisions taken are much more likely to be based on political factors than economic or efficiency factors.

For investors the key point to remember here is that any moves in the direction of free trade imply faster growth for the countries involved (especially the country liberalising) and lower prices or slower inflation in the country liberalising. Conversely moves towards protectionism tend to mean higher inflation and slower growth.

The politics of trade

In practice trade has become a very hot political issue, with powerful lobby groups both for protectionism and for liberalisation and a strong popular involvement in the issues. Some economists have argued that there is a bias towards protectionism although fortunately there are forces in favour of liberalising as well. Let's list both sides:

Firstly there is a bias towards protection because individual interest groups protecting a particular industry are often able to powerfully influence politicians while the consumers who would gain from continuing free trade are dispersed and unorganised. For example the heavy protection of the US and European car industries in the 1980s was to the benefit of car producers, enabling jobs, incomes and profits to be held while to the rest of the population prices of cars were much higher than they need be. But the 95% of the population who suffered was only partly aware of it and in any case suffered less than an individual car worker or company would have suffered. Politicians are able to draw their own conclusions from this equation.

Secondly if a country has a trade deficit then the people perceiving themselves to be suffering from imports are likely to be a bigger lobby group than the people who perceive themselves as gaining from exports and so there may be bias towards protection.

Thirdly there is a view, notably in the current US administration, that one way to expand exports to countries with real or perceived barriers is to threaten to cut imports. Most economists are ambivalent on this. If the net result is greater trade all round then everybody is happy. If however the threats have to be put in to play, the result would be worse. The policy is therefore dangerous and is not necessarily in the interests of the country trying it. It is important to remember that the benefits of freeing imports are felt primarily by the country doing the liberalisation, not by other countries. Lower domestic prices and more competition for domestic producers forces efficiency gains and makes everybody better off.

On the positive side, there are an increasing number of multinational companies and banks who regard free and liberal trade as important for their business. The more that companies outsource their parts, and this applies to service companies as well as manufacturing companies, and the more that companies produce in a variety of countries, the more they are in favour of freeing trade.

Finally there is a very powerful ideological case for free trade, traditionally carried by the US Presidency and some other countries including the UK and Germany. This is reinforced by the historical memory of the problems in the 1930s which were partly caused by the resort to protectionism in the face of world recession.

Capital Flows

As we have seen, in the modern world of free capital movements it is increasingly the net flows of capital, caused by savings-investment imbalances which drive the exchange rate. There are three broad reasons behind private capital flows. *Firstly*, relative interest rates and yields generally, e.g. on stocks, are frequently a crucial factor. Countries with high rates and yields will attract an inflow. In the mid-1980s the USA was an outstanding example of this as high interest rates and bond yields attracted massive inflows and drove the dollar up. Other high interest rate currencies such as Australia and Canada in the late 1980s also enjoyed massive inflows.

Of course, if investors see high yields but worry about exchange rate depreciation then they may buy bonds or stocks but hedge the currency. The effect of the hedging is to offset the inflow of capital associated with buying the bond so that there is no net inflow. This will register in the balance of payments as an inflow of long-term capital and an outflow of short-term capital.

Secondly, countries with low exchange rates may attract an inflow, even with only moderate interest rates, because investors expect a currency appreciation. The US dollar seems to have benefited from this in 1993 and early 1994. What may be happening sometimes is not so much that investors flock into deposits and wait for the currency to appreciate but investors who already hold bonds or stocks remove hedges because the balance of risk has shifted with the currency low. The effect of removing a hedge is equivalent to an inflow of capital.

Finally, some capital flows are relatively unaffected by interest rates or exchange rates and reflect long term or structural factors. For example the attractiveness of dollars as a currency to hold or as a means of payment, throughout the world but particularly in Latin America and eastern Europe, means that the US can enjoy a continuous effective inflow. Some of the dollars spent by Americans on imports stay out there rather than coming back to pay for US exports. Another structural flow is direct investment. Although it is not unaffected by interest rates and exchange rates, some of it is mainly driven by other factors.

All these capital flows are on the increase as capital controls are removed and international investment becomes increasingly important. Of course for most countries flows are increasing in both directions. Only the net inflows or outflows impact on exchange rates.

7. International Interactions and Policy Coordination

Overview

Direct Economic Impacts

Is there a world business cycle?
Will cycles converge again?
The international impact of oil prices
Oil now just another commodity

Market Linkages

Interest rate linkages
What determines the interest differential?
Linkages in bond yields
1. Through exchange rate expectations
Three examples
2. Through world capital flows
Stock markets linkages

Policy Coordination

World coordination to boost economic growth
Currency manipulation
How does intervention work?

Overview

Economic and market trends in one country often impact on other countries. Investors have to take account of three types of interactions: direct economic interactions between the business cycles in different countries, market interactions through linkages in bond, stock and currency markets and efforts at economic policy coordination, for example by the G7 countries.

Direct Economic Impacts

Is there a world business cycle?

It is no accident that recessions and booms often seem to come more or less at the same time in different countries. Faster economic growth in one country (especially if it is large) stimulates the exports of another. The rise in exports lifts the whole economy as investment increases and incomes pick up. In recent years these trends have been particularly noticeable in Europe. For example in the early 1990s the German reunification boom lifted growth in most of continental Europe in 1990-1 while in 1994 continental European countries emerged from recession together. It has also been noticeable in Asia in recent years where strong Chinese growth has stimulated the surrounding countries.

Similarly, a slowdown in one economy is likely to impact elsewhere too. Part of the impact may come directly through affecting exports and therefore incomes and business confidence in the second country. To this may be added the market linkages and policy coordination linkages discussed below.

But business cycles are far from completely synchronised and in recent years have been less so than previously. For example the last US recession ended in spring 1991 whereas Germany and Japan only emerged from recession in 1994. A glance at the chart overleaf suggests that after being closely coordinated in the 1970s the European and US cycles have returned to the situation of the 1960s where they were not coordinated.

There would seem to be two reasons for this reversal. Firstly, the synchronisation in the previous major recessions, 1974-5 and 1981-2, was due primarily to the world-wide impact of higher oil prices. Secondly, Continental Europe grew strongly in 1990-1, despite the temporary rise in oil prices that year and the recession in the English-speaking countries, because of the one-off impact of German unification.

The Business Cycle in Germany and The USA

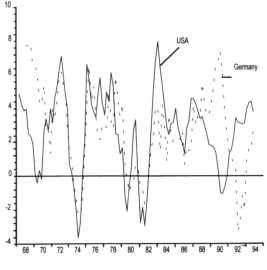

Source: DATASTREAM

Will cycles converge again?

Some people believe that the current divergence in business cycles is just a temporary aberration caused by German unification. With international trade growing and the world economy becoming more integrated the world business cycle should converge over time. However it could also be argued that the dominance of the United States in the world economy is in steady decline and therefore its leadership role in the world economy is dwindling. Forty years ago the United States accounted for two-thirds of world GDP. Now the figure is less than one-third. As Europe integrates further and countries' economies move closer together, Europe's relative weight becomes more important for the rest of the world. Hence we may be moving towards a "multi-polar" world economy with the USA, Europe and Asia moving separately.

The more trade that a country has with another the more its economic cycle becomes converged. For example the impact of the German unification boom in Europe was greatest for those countries already exporting a great deal to Germany, notably Austria, Switzerland, Holland and France but less important for countries such as the UK which had a smaller proportion of exports going to Germany.

The international impact of oil prices

Economic developments everywhere in the 1970s and 1980s were dominated by movements in the world oil price. For the most part oil prices were moved by long-term changes in supply and demand though the OPEC cartel was also influential at certain key times, most notably in 1973-4.

In the early 1970s demand for oil had risen to more or less equal total available supply. When OPEC quadrupled prices in 1973 the rise was sustainable because the oil market was so tight. But for industrial countries the extra money being paid to oil producers amounted to a withdrawal of 2-3% of GDP. Higher oil prices also sent consumer prices rocketing up. The result was to plunge the industrial countries virtually simultaneously into a severe recession thereby synchronising the world business cycle. The re-doubling of prices in 1979 had a similar effect.

In the mid-1980s the situation had reversed. As a result of the price rises in 1973 and again in 1979 the demand for oil had risen much more slowly than supply so that there was clear over-capacity in the market. In 1986 OPEC was unable to agree on lower production quotas and the oil price responded by halving in the course of a few weeks. This decline was very important for the continuation of the world economic upswing until the late 1980s. Without the benefit of the downward impetus to inflation from lower oil prices, the central banks in many countries would have brought the 1980s upswing to an end much earlier.

The rise in oil prices in 1990 after Iraq's invasion of Kuwait impacted on business expectations everywhere. In the English-speaking countries recessions were already beginning and the oil price rise converted a moderate downturn into a sharp fall in output. For continental Europe though, the unification boom was too strong to be derailed by oil prices.

Oil now just another commodity

Energy conservation and diversification away from oil mean that oil prices are no longer the frightening force they once were. Only a major political event, probably in the Middle East, would prompt a new crisis. Nevertheless oil and oil products still account for around half of the value of raw commodities. So if oil prices rise, even moderately, they will take commodity indices up and may impact on inflation and interest rates.

The prices of non-oil commodities also played a role in the world cycle in the 1970s and 1980s, though the swings in price and consequently the impact was much less dramatic. Prices of metals and food rose during the 1970s and fell in real terms during the 1980s, reflecting world supply and demand. When they were rising in the 1970s they contributed to the upward trend in inflation while in the 1980s weak commodity prices were a factor in restraining inflation in the industrial countries. In 1994-5 industrial commodity prices rose in response to strong growth but oil prices remained relatively flat.

Market Linkages

Interest rate linkages

Short term interest rates are very often affected by developments in other countries because the central bank is pursuing a formal or informal exchange rate link. Sometimes two or more countries are deliberately trying to coordinate policy to influence exchange rates. The Exchange Rate Mechanism in Europe is a good example and is discussed in more detail in section 3 below. But even without *mutual* policy coordination many governments *unilaterally* peg their currencies firmly or loosely to one of the major currencies, usually the US dollar or Deutschemark. The Canadian authorities, for example, have followed an interest rate policy linked to US policy. If Canada cuts its short term rates then the Canadian dollar will usually decline. If the authorities feel that the exchange rate is falling too quickly then they raise rates to steady it.

The advantages for countries who follow this strategy are two-fold. *Firstly,* it provides business with some comfort that exchange rates are not going to fluctuate wildly. Of course, instead, short-term interest rates may very well fluctuate wildly! *Secondly*, by pegging the exchange rate the country often hopes to control inflation. This has been particularly important in Europe where pegging to the Deutschemark either formally or informally has been widespread in recent years and has contributed to the general downtrend in European inflation.

What determines the interest differential?

Ultimately, if a country is sticking rigidly to an exchange rate policy then the level of interest rates necessary will depend on overall market confidence in policy. If there is a high degree of confidence that the exchange rate will stick then interest rates can converge to near zero, as has occurred in the Netherlands, or France before 1992. If the markets see the policy as unsustainable and expect that the exchange rate may be devalued then they will demand a substantial interest differential.

Some countries do not have a rigid policy but nevertheless do treat the exchange rate as a target. For example the Bank of Canada has several times sharply raised interest rates in recent years to defend the Canadian dollar but has not prevented it from first rising strongly between 1986 and 1991 and then declining 20% after December 1991. The Bank's approach is to treat interest rates and the currency as two aspects of monetary conditions. If the currency falls then monetary conditions will have eased, unless the decline is offset by a rise in interest rates. The Bank decides on monetary conditions according to its assessment of the inflation outlook, and then balances interest rates and the currency to achieve the desired monetary conditions.

Linkages in bond yields

Although the government can directly control short term interest rates, bond yields are not directly in its control. Nevertheless bond yields in different countries are connected, through two routes: exchange rate expectations and capital flows.

1. Through exchange rate expectations

If a country is known to be linking its currency to another, then bond yields of the weaker currency are linked to the strongest currency and are nearly always higher. Hence in Europe the bond yields of France and the UK are watched by the markets as a spread over German bond yields. If the expectation is that the French franc/DM exchange rate will remain broadly the same as its current level over the long term, either because of the government's determination to maintain a parity or because the market assessment of inflation and competitiveness in France is such that there is no need for a devaluation, then bond yields in France will converge on Germany. They could be less than

German yields, if either the market decides that the fundamentals in France are so good that the French franc is now a fundamentally stronger currency or if the French franc has been depressed against the DM to an artificially low level and therefore is likely to appreciate.

Bond Yields in France and Germany

Source: DATASTREAM

Similarly the markets analyse Canadian bonds in relation to US bonds. Yields have converged to a smaller premium over the US in recent years. This reflects a view that the risk of Canadian dollar depreciation has dwindled as the Canadian inflation rate has fallen below US levels and also the exchange rate in Canada has moved down substantially from its high levels of the early 1990s.

However, even if countries are not trying to link their currencies, this connection between exchange rate expectations and bond yields means that bond yields can diverge substantially between countries. For example, if one country's exchange rate is expected to rise substantially against another country's, then bond yields will be relatively lower than they would otherwise be in relation to the other country. In effect bond holders know that the appreciation in the currency can offset developments in interest rates. This obviously works the other way around too, where if a country's exchange rate is likely to depreciate substantially then the bond markets will require an extra premium to hold those bonds.

Three examples

Exchange rates could be over or under-valued requiring an offset from bond yields for a number of reasons. One possibility is that government action on *short-term* interest rates has affected exchange rates. For example the Exchange Rate Mechanism was maintained as long as it was by using high short term interest rates to limit speculation against currencies.

Another example is the UK in 1993. After leaving the ERM the UK government reduced short term interest rates faster than the Bundesbank which had the effect of taking Sterling to a level which was widely seen as undervalued against the Deutschmark and therefore leaving the possibility of appreciation. In that environment gilts yields could decline relative to German bond yields because the bond market anticipated a possible currency rise.

A final example is where bond yields are pushed up by a particularly strong economy. In 1984 US bond yields averaged 12.5% versus inflation of 4%. This high real and nominal rate was due to the combination of the US budget deficit raising demands for borrowing and a strong private sector economy as the US rebounded vigorously from the early 1980s recession. In comparison, Germany had bond yields of 8% with inflation of 2.5%. Hence investors in the US could enjoy real yields 3% p.a. above investors in German bunds. This was enough to take the dollar up substantially in 1983-85, leaving the markets in some degree of equilibrium. Although there was a widespread expectation that the dollar would have to come down, long term investors in bonds were enjoying the yield advantage.

2. Through world capital flows

Obviously *nominal* bond yields vary between countries according to their different inflation outlooks and other factors. It is sometimes thought that *real* bond yields, i.e. after inflation ought to be similar in different countries because international capital flows will equalise them. But as we have seen movements in exchange rates to under or over valued levels can compensate for different real bond yields so real bond yields can vary.

However although they *can* and often do vary there is nevertheless a tendency for them to move together. In the example above from 1984 bond yields in *both* the USA and Germany were comparatively high in relation to inflation and either prior or more recent experience.

The key factor linking bond yields (especially real bond yields) is world supply and demand for capital or the perception of it. For example in 1994 the collapse of world bond markets and the sharp rise in bond yields seems to have been partly due to a perception that synchronised world growth, combined with large budget deficits would force short and long term interest rates up as the demand for world savings exceeded the supply. Since in the end the demand has to equal the supply, interest rates everywhere rose to choke off demand and/or stimulate more supply.

Stock market linkages

There is plenty of evidence that stock markets are linked and to some extent move together. For example calculations show that 59% of the movement of the UK's stock market index can be accounted for by movements in the US index *(see table)*. The other 41% reflects other factors including domestic issues and European factors. The reason for these linkages is partly links through trade and the business cycle but also the fact that many UK companies make substantial profits overseas. Around half of the profits of the 100 top UK companies in the FTSE index come from abroad.

Correlations between stock markets

	USA	UK	Japan	Mexico	Korea
USA	1				
UK	0.59	1			
Japan	0.31	0.49	1		
Mexico	0.40	0.23	0.16	1	
Korea	0.23	0.34	0.34	0.29	1

Source: International Finance Corporation

After the 1987 stock market crash when most markets fell substantially in response to the initial decline in the United States, it appeared as though the stock markets themselves could be a transmission mechanism for business confidence around the world. When many of those markets recovered in the following few months this view lost credibility.

The extent to which stock markets are correlated is an important issue for investors. By holding a mix of different markets, investors can smooth out annual returns and face less risk of a large drop in any one year. Moreover in time this translates into higher returns. This is why professional investors actively look for shares and markets which are uncorrelated with their core holdings.

Policy Coordination

In the last 20 years policy coordination has generally focused around two problems, currency management and boosting economic growth. In contrast, governments have not tried hard to coordinate when the emphasis has been on slowing economic growth to reduce inflation, seeing that problem as primarily an internal one.

Episodes of policy coordination tend to go in fits and starts. Coordination to boost world growth naturally comes up during recession periods. Currency coordination is most prevalent when the dollar is especially weak. The extent to which the coordination is real and the extent to which it is primarily rhetoric varies. There seems little doubt that G7 summit meetings have become at least as much a way to play to home electorates as to make hard agreements on policy coordination. Nevertheless there has been an increasing degree of discussion on policy coordination and particularly on the currency front. Moreover there is evidence that currency coordination has been more successful in the 1980s than it was in the early 1970s.

World coordination to boost economic growth

Often one or more countries in recession wants stronger growth elsewhere to help their exports but they are afraid of too much stimulation at home for fear of accelerating inflation. However the experience of countries which have helped out in supplying this growth has been mixed. The most celebrated example was Germany in the late 1970s which deliberately boosted growth to help support the world economy. Unfortunately this stimulus came just before the second oil price shock and the result was a sharp rise in German inflation and a serious deterioration in the public finances. German officials vowed never again.

Japan's efforts to support the dollar and simultaneously boost the Japanese economy in 1987 also ended in tears. By 1989 the Bank of Japan was bitterly regretting the asset price boom that followed the monetary stimulus and desperately trying to cool it. The most successful example of one country leading the world was the United States in 1983-4. However this was not policy coordination - the US economy took off on its own because of tax cuts and interest rate reductions and other countries just enjoyed the ride.

It is doubtful now whether individual countries are prepared to take on the burden of boosting growth unless they are quite sure it fits in with their own objectives and in particular does not clash with their inflation objectives. Nevertheless coordination can be important where world business confidence is low. A convincing coordinated move by governments to stimulate across the board can have a significant impact. The nearest we have come to this is the few months immediately following the October 1987 stock market crash when governments and central banks everywhere combined to stimulate their economies in the face of what was seen as the danger of a slump.

Currency manipulation

Since the world moved to floating rates in the early 1970s there have been periodic attempts to control exchange rates. But economists and the markets have been sceptical whether governments really can control them with market intervention alone.

Scepticism over the ability of governments to control exchange rates stems from three factors. *Firstly,* we know that the total value of foreign exchange trading is in excess of 1 trillion dollars *daily*. This is about three times the total foreign exchange reserves of the major central banks. *Secondly,* most economists believe that market prices are determined by fundamentals and so governments, however big they are, just another player. *Thirdly*, experience with trying to control foreign exchange trends prior to the 1980s was not promising even with the widespread capital controls then in place. Most participants concluded that, unless governments were prepared to move interest rates and perhaps change other policies as well as intervene in the markets, then they could not expect to succeed.

How does intervention work?

When a government buys its own currency using its foreign exchange reserves the effect is to reduce the amount of domestic currency in the country. This would normally raise interest rates by reducing the supply of funds and so if the government does nothing else then the currency benefits from the rise in interest rates. This is what is known as unsterilised intervention and this kind of intervention is usually seen as likely to be successful because interest rates move too.

However very often governments seek to offset the effect on interest rates by sterilising the foreign exchange market intervention. This is done by matching the reduction in local currency resulting from the FX market intervention by buying back Treasury bills or other paper, thereby putting money back into the economy. From the government's point of view this has the advantage that interest rates do not rise. It is this kind of sterilised intervention which, by the late 1980s, was generally seen as likely to be unsuccessful.

However the experience of the G7 countries in the late 1980s and early 1990s has suggested that, even with sterilised intervention, governments can at times influence exchange rates by impacting on market expectations. One reason may be that central banks have intervened in a coordinated way so that every bank is in the market at the same time.

Another effective technique has been to have relatively vague currency ranges, and not to publicise exactly what they are. If a range has hard edges and is known to the markets, then once the exchange rate moves beyond the edge, the government loses all credibility (as was seen with the collapse of the Exchange Rate Mechanism in 1992/3). If however the edges are soft then governments can intervene more and more as the exchange rate goes away from the level they want, but there is no single point where governments are clearly defeated.

A third factor is that foreign exchange markets like to have reasons for picking certain levels for the currency. It makes life easier if they can feel that a currency is particularly weak or particularly strong and that in itself sets up factors taking currency back to the middle.

The success of G7 intervention in this period, however, may not last. The markets tasted blood during the collapse of the Exchange Rate Mechanism in 1992-3 and also at around the same time forced the Canadian dollar and Australian dollar to levels which were lower than the governments hoped for. The sharp decline in the US dollar in early 1995 occurred despite coordinated intervention. It may be argued that the period of the late 1980s and early 1990s actually did see a convergence of economic policy to a significant extent which allowed exchange rates to trade within a narrower range. This is in contrast to the 1970s and early 1980s when policy was more divergent. In the mid 1990s, with economic cycles desynchronised, G7 intervention may again be needed.

8. Theories of Investment

Investing in Value

The use of benchmarks

Are Markets "Efficient"?

A random walk
The efficient markets' hypothesis (EMH)
Are markets really efficient?

Approaches Based on Risk

What do we mean by risk?
The capital asset pricing model (CAPM)
Beta and the investor
The arbitrage pricing theory model (APT)
Efficient markets and the investor

The Performance of Different Asset Classes

There are two broad approaches to investment. One is to look for value, for example cheap stocks or undervalued asset classes. The second approach, which is based on theories developed over the last 40 years, is to focus on risk, return and correlations between different securities or asset classes. Using this approach the investor can build a portfolio of stocks, bonds, etc. based on a careful analysis of their past behaviour. This second approach follows from the "efficient markets hypothesis" which states that markets are efficient and therefore investors cannot generally beat them. In practice most investors use a combination of both approaches but it is useful to consider them separately in order to understand the fundamental bases of the two approaches.

Investing in Value

For many investors, both private and institutional, value is to be found by searching for company stocks or fixed income securities which are under-rated by the markets or where the investor feels the market may not be anticipating fully the potential for that company or industry. For stocks or corporate bonds a disciplined approach requires both a careful analysis of the financials of that company and a close understanding of the company's management and business. Investment in international government bonds requires analysis of economic trends such as inflation and economic growth.

Another approach to value investing is called market timing. If investors can be positioned in stock markets just before economic recovery begins and move out near the top of the upswing and into bonds just as the downswing begins, then they can gain with the rise in the stock market and then gain further with the rise in the bond market! If investors can time things internationally as well then, in theory it is possible to move in and out and always enjoy the best performing markets around the world!

The reality of course is that this is much more difficult than it sounds because of the huge uncertainties at every stage of the business cycle. Even if investors correctly judge the business cycle, markets often seem to behave perversely, moving up when they might be expected to go down and vice-versa!

The danger is not just the obvious one of being caught in a market (or overweight a market) when it is going down but also of being out of a market when it goes up. For example the S&P index in the United States rose 68% in the five years to January 1st 1994. The clever (or lucky) investor who moved into cash for the whole of 1990, the recession year when the S&P moved down 8%, would have enjoyed an increased return, around 90%. But the nervous investor who was *out* of the market in *either* 1989 or 1991, both years when the S&P surged 28%, would have seen a five year return of only about 35% instead of 68%, no better than the return on deposits over that period.

The use of benchmarks

Most professional investors are very careful not to use market timing to put all their eggs in one basket but instead, use it to change their portfolio weightings in a small way. They start with a benchmark, usually a widely quoted index, e.g. the Morgan Stanley Capital International (MSCI) stock indices or the Salomon brothers bond indices, but it could be a specially constructed one. These indices are based on the value of shares or bonds outstanding in each market. Then they make departures from the benchmark weighting according to their view of the markets.

For example suppose that the Benchmark weighting for US stocks is 40% of the portfolio. If the investor believes that the US economy is approaching a recession and therefore US stock prices are likely to fall then they may go down to 30% or perhaps lower. But only a very aggressive fund would go down to near zero.

With this kind of approach the choice of the right benchmark is as important as the choice of stocks within the portfolio. For example using the Dow Jones stock index as a benchmark would imply that the stocks picked are likely to be large blue-chip companies. Or if the portfolio is to be "balanced", i.e. include both stocks and bonds, then as we shall see below the proportions of stocks and bonds in the benchmark will be a key determinant of the portfolio's risk and return, unless the manager departs from the benchmark in substantial ways.

Are Markets "Efficient"?

Since the 1950s there has been a growing literature on how markets work and whether clever investors really can make money through value investing. Much of this work has centred around the so-called "efficient markets hypothesis" or EMH. The key argument of the EMH is that the markets are "efficient" in the sense that they incorporate all the information available and therefore it is not possible to beat the market.

A random walk

The starting point is the observation, based on numerous academic studies, that markets follow a "random walk". That is they are just as likely to go up as down in any one time period. Imagine a drunk walking along a street slowly. Each step could take him either to the left or right but it is impossible to be sure until he has made it.

To many people the random walk idea seems very surprising because markets do show clear trends over time while charts of markets seem to show very clear patterns. For more than 100 years analysts have been trying to use these patterns and trends to predict the next move. Numerous theories have been put forward and many so-called chartists have developed complex ways of analysing markets.

But the theorists have shown that even random

events can produce charts like this. Try tossing a coin 20 times; each time it comes up heads draw a small line diagonally up to the right and when it comes up tails draw a small line diagonally down to the right. The result often looks remarkably like a market chart!

Despite the widespread acceptance of the "Random Walk" hypothesis in academic circles there are still numerous chartists for both stock markets and other markets. Should they be dismissed entirely? This is a difficult question. A Bank of England study of chartists on currency markets discovered that most of the chartists' forecasts were no better than a random forecast but one chartist in particular (who was unnamed) did startlingly better than simply tossing a coin!

Another reason for not completely rejecting chartism is that if enough people believe in chart points then they may indeed have a special significance. To take an example, suppose chartists claim that 4300 is a crucial breakpoint on the Dow Jones index and if the market goes below that level it will fall substantially more. If enough people believe this it is likely to become a self-fulfilling prophecy. Many professional investment managers do use chartists' services, usually to look at short term trends or to see where current prices are in relation to recent trading ranges.

The efficient markets hypothesis (EMH)

The random walk theory tries to discredit chartists. An extension of it, called the efficient markets hypothesis (EMH), tries to do the same thing for fundamentals analysis! According to the EMH the market price of a stock, or any other asset, already takes into account all the known information and reasonable expectations about the future.

This theory goes much farther than the random walk hypothesis in saying not only that investors cannot use past patterns or trends in prices to predict future movements but that even a clever investor with good access to information cannot know more than the market already knows. If the price of a share differs from its real value even for a short time, so the theory goes, arbitragers will move in to buy or sell the security and bring it back to its fair price.

It is as though a Chinese restaurateur thinking of opening a new restaurant is told that he could not possibly make money because there is already a Chinese restaurant in every town and the market for Chinese restaurants is in equilibrium. Most people would reject this argument and would anticipate that an astute restaurateur, choosing his location well and running his restaurant effectively, could certainly make a profit. Taking the analogy to the financial markets though, remember that the market is much bigger and more uniform than the market for Chinese meals, where every location is unique and that therefore the inefficiencies that may exist in the restaurant market may be much reduced in the securities market.

Are markets really efficient?

There have been numerous attempts to test the efficient markets hypothesis over the past 25 years and generally researchers have confirmed it, except for limited cases. There is evidence for example of gains to be made by buying stocks with low PE ratios or by buying small stocks or by investing early in January (the so-called January effect). On the whole most academic studies treat these as small exceptions, from which it would be difficult to make money in practice. Many academics therefore take the efficient markets hypothesis to be true.

However there are a number of objections to it:

1. Why do people try to beat the market if they cannot? The efficient markets hypothesis suggests that investors and their advisors are wasting their time in trying to analyse markets and securities. But that would make investors "irrational" and if investors are irrational then a great deal of economic theory is in trouble. Not least the view, implicit in the EMH, that the markets are in fact

pricing assets efficiently and thereby helping to ensure that capital goes to the right place. Put another way, if every investor believed that markets were efficient then the market could not be efficient since no-one would analyse securities!

2. The costly information argument. In its simplest form the efficient markets hypothesis assumes that everybody has the same information. However information is not freely available to everybody and nor is its careful analysis. Investors who spend a lot of time and money acquiring and analysing information, whether they are professional or private investors, ought to be able to do better than the market.

3. This objection is usually shot down by believers in the efficient markets hypothesis by pointing to studies which suggest that on average professional investment managers do no better than the market, and indeed often on average do worse. However, other studies contradict these findings and suggest that an investment house that has done well over one period is likely to continue to do well over the next period. This would seem to accord with most people's view of the world in general, i.e. that there are smart hard-working people who can often do better than other people.

4. If investors have differing abilities and often different knowledge, how can markets be efficient? The EMH appears to be making great claims when it argues that markets are good at pricing assets. Some academics argue that it is possible because the unskilled investors will lose money and drop out of the markets leaving it to the skilled investors. Talented investors will remain in the market and arbitrage out any mis-pricing. However this does not seem really plausible. Many people with money are indeed hiring professionals to manage it for them but there still appears to be a range of talent active in the marketplace.

Some more recent studies by academics have focused on the possibility that there are two types of investors in the market, one type who follows fundamentals and another who follows fashions or jumps onto trends. It has been shown that the market will still appear to follow a random walk hypothesis even with these assumptions.

Most professional investors do not accept the efficient markets hypothesis in total but they do draw a number of conclusions for practical investment. *Firstly*, as explained above, they are cautious of making big bets on one stock or one market because of the danger of being wrong. *Secondly*, they are wary of buying and selling too actively within a portfolio. If it is difficult to beat the market, then racking up heavy costs in turning over the portfolio means that the fund is liable to under-perform. *Finally*, and perhaps most importantly, the theory emphasises the importance of diversifying.

Approaches Based on Risk

The efficient markets hypothesis leads on to theories of investment based on risk, which collectively are known as modern portfolio theory (MPT).

What do we mean by risk?

In modern portfolio theory, risk is defined as the volatility of the price of a security over a period. If the average daily or weekly movement of one stock up and down is greater than another, i.e. it is more volatile, then it is seen as having higher risk. At first sight this definition of risk may seem odd. After all the long term investor is interested in the long term return and whether or not the company might perform very badly or go bankrupt. The fact that the share price is volatile should not necessarily matter very much.

However volatility *is* a negative factor for an investor. If he needs to sell up for some reason he could lose out if the stock has lurched down sharply, even if the fall is only temporary. Still, this only leads to the conclusion that a proportion of investments should be held in low volatility securities in case the investor needs money suddenly.

But the real reason that volatility matters is that, over time, the scale of movements in a stock price relative to the market are indicative of the stock's basic riskiness. Suppose a company is very vulnerable to the price of oil, and might go bust if oil prices fell below $10. Small movements in the oil price from week to week of only a few cents, as the markets react to news, are likely to move that stock price significantly up or down, and are thus indicating that the stock is risky because of its dependence on one factor. Investors know that it is vulnerable and so they will buy or sell at a moment's notice for only small changes in the relevant factors. In contrast a company which does not have such a vulnerability to the oil price or to any other major factors, for example a large diversified company, will naturally respond less dramatically to news. Hence the short term volatility of any security is an indicator of riskiness.

The capital asset pricing model (CAPM)

Although this model can become quite complicated, the basic idea is fairly simple. What it says is that the return on a stock comes from two sources, the rise in the market itself and the return of the stock compared to the market, known as beta. The beta of a particular stock represents the ratio of the average movement of the stock price over a specific period compared with the overall market index. For example if, when the market moves 1% up or down, this stock typically moves by 2% in the same direction then it will have a beta of 2. Large company stocks in diversified industries will tend to have a beta close to 1 indicating that they tend to move more or less up and down with the market. Utility stocks will tend to move less than the market and therefore will have a beta between 0 and 1. Smaller stocks are often more volatile and have a beta greater than 1. Some stocks of course may be negatively correlated so that when the market rises they tend to fall. Beta is then negative.

Beta and the investor

What does this mean for the investor? The key point is that to obtain above average returns the investor will need to take above average risks. While, if the investor is reluctant to take risk then potential returns are going to be limited. A related point is that if a fund (mutual fund for example) is showing high returns historically this could be because it has a high beta, i.e. is taking a lot of risk. That is fine, but it means that next year's performance could be strongly negative. Some funds now publish their beta levels in order to indicate what sort of risk investors are facing. Very often funds that are described as "aggressive" or "growth" or "smaller company" will have a beta greater than the market. Over the long run, 3-5 years or more, they should outperform but it may be more of a rollercoaster than the market.

Professional investors use beta to balance a portfolio to make sure that it is taking the risk they want relative to the market. For example suppose they have identified some stocks they like (on value grounds) but find that the combined beta is 1½ then by choosing another set of stocks with a lower beta the portfolio's overall risk could be reduced.

Notice that the approach here differs from the value approach discussed above. Whereas value investors are trying deliberately to outperform the market, investors using the capital asset pricing model start from the supposition that they can only outperform the market by taking higher risk.

In practice beta has run into difficulties which have led many to question its usefulness. The main problem is that it varies over time. Hence carefully constructing a portfolio based on beta calculated over the last five years (for example) may not give the returns expected, in future.

The arbitrage pricing theory model (APT)

This theory, which was first formalised in the late 1970s, is much more complex than the CAPM but is more realistic. In simple terms it says that a stock's risk can be broken down into a range of factors, not just its own risk relative to the market and the market risk (as in the CAPM). This range of factors includes industry exposure, movements in the business cycle, changes in inflation and changes in the yield curve among others. These risks may not be possible to eliminate through diversification and therefore will affect all stocks though in different proportions.

Hence in this theory, instead of coming up with a single beta which is the risk attached to the market, a whole series of coefficients of risk can be derived from different economic or market events. Using the theory in its most developed form, an investor could buy a set of stocks deliberately designed to benefit from a rise in oil prices, a fall in interest rates and a rise in industrial production, without this having any relation to the businesses the stocks are in. This development is sometimes known as the components approach.

These are sophisticated attempts to manage investments and are generally beyond the scope of the private investor. Note that many professional investors who use these approaches are not accepting the academics' view that it is impossible to beat the market. Instead they are using the models to make absolutely sure that they know what the market expects and then, where their judgement differs from the market, taking a measured bet against the market.

Efficient markets and the investor

Where does all this leave the private investor? A number of conclusions can be drawn. *Firstly* modern portfolio theory demonstrates the importance of understanding the relationship between risk and return. Generally speaking, investments which are likely to provide a higher return are likely to have more risk. That means that they will have bad years that are worse than other investments and good years that are better, but over the long term, which for stocks should be 3 to 5 years or more, they will outperform.

Secondly it is vital to diversify if the objective is to preserve wealth. The important point is that the investor concerned to see his portfolio grow steadily needs to be in a wide range of stocks and a wide range of asset classes *(see below)*.

Thirdly while investors can choose how active to be in the markets the EMH suggests that the best strategy is to buy and hold. Frequent trading costs money and may not improve returns.

Most investors in practice seem to divide up their resources into three parts. *Firstly* there is a part which they are particularly anxious should remain safe, secure and liquid, partly because they feel they might need it in the near term and partly because they want it absolutely safe. Note though that cash is not necessarily the safest place if inflation picks up. The real value of deposits can fall rapidly in high inflation as many people found to their cost in the 1970s.

Secondly there is another part of their wealth which they would like to have under management, over time doing significantly better than cash and sufficiently diversified to avoid being dependent on one market only. That money is often put in mutual funds or individually tailored portfolios.

Finally many investors, though not all, have a third part of their wealth, typically only a small proportion, which is under their own direct management and where they follow their own views or advisors' ideas on good investments. For some people managing these investments is a hobby as much as anything. Nevertheless it is also where the investor finds out more about the markets and is able to monitor his professionally managed funds more closely.

The Performance of Different Asset Classes

The next three chapters in this book look at bonds, stocks and currency markets in more detail but it is important to understand the basic relationships between these different asset classes when building a total portfolio. In simple terms, the general rule is that over time (and in this context time is measured in 5-10 years or more) stocks will outperform bonds and bonds will do better than cash. The basis for this assertion is both the historical record and theory.

Firstly, the historical record. Taking the United States, since 1900 on average, stocks have returned 6-7% per annum above inflation, and government bonds have returned about 1% more than inflation, slightly ahead of Treasury bills. Similar numbers can be found in the UK. However it should be noted that there are exceptions. Bonds performed particularly badly for many years in the 1970s while stocks performed badly in the 1930s and again in the 1970s. In Germany bonds outperformed stocks for more than 15 years in the 1970s and early 1980s. Nevertheless, taking the very long run, these are the exceptions.

Secondly, the theoretical reasons. The investor is taking more risk by holding bonds rather than cash and more risk again by holding stocks rather than bonds. Holding bonds involves the risk of unexpected inflation and/or a change in short term interest rates which would reduce the value of the holding. Investors in stocks face the risk of bankruptcy of that company or of earnings underperforming expectations.

The difference between the return on stocks and the return on bonds is known as the equity premium and there is some evidence that, whereas it used to be 5-6% p.a. (in line with the figures above), it has been declining over time. There is less agreement on exactly why this should be so. Certainly investors who bought stocks during the 1950s or again during the early 1980s would have done extraordinarily well, but in recent years bonds have offered returns similar to stocks in many major markets. It may be that this reflects the strong disinflation of the early 1990s. If this period of declining inflation is now over, stocks will again tend to outperform bonds, in line with both theory and historical experience.

9. Currency Markets

Introduction

Can exchange rates be forecasted?
Three key concepts
Covered interest parity
Real exchange rate

Forecasting Approaches

1. Fundamental or equilibrium exchange rates
Calculating purchasing power parity
Why PPP is still relevant
The Yen and PPP: why Tokyo is so expensive
2. Relative economic strength
Combining PPP with relative strength

Government Intervention

Does G7 intervention work?
The European Exchange Rate Mechanism
Is EMU feasible?
Conclusion: exchange rates and investors

For international investors exchange rates represent both risk and opportunity since movements in exchange rates are frequently much greater than gains or losses in individual bonds or stocks over short time periods. Exchange rates can often be explained by relative inflation trends (through changes in so-called purchasing power parities) or by relative economic strength (through changes in real interest rates). But forecasting, as opposed to explaining after the event, is not easy. A cautious approach to currencies is well advised, because of the risks involved. One factor to watch is government intervention. Experience suggests that governments trying to defend overvalued exchange rates usually are forced to give way in the end. But in recent years government intervention to support the dollar when it has become undervalued or sell it when it looks strong has often been successful.

Introduction

Can exchange rates be forecasted?

Academic economists argue that the currency markets (like other markets) are "efficient" in the sense that they include all the available information. In fact since the markets in the major currencies are so liquid and enjoy very low transaction costs they are believed to be the most efficient of markets. This implies that exchange rates are impossible to forecast *(see chapter 8)*. Most professional investors do not fully accept the "efficient markets hypothesis" but would certainly agree that exchange rates are very hard to forecast.

The problem is that currencies seem to behave differently at different times. In the 1980s monthly US trade reports were the key to fluctuations in the dollar. At other times interest rates have been the key factor. There have been still other times when the markets seem to have been gripped by so-called "fads or fashions", taking exchange rates to dizzyingly high or stunningly low levels.

There are a number of forecasting models around but they only work if other variables are correctly forecast and sometimes not even then. For example in 1992-3 there was general agreement that a strong US employment report would boost the dollar because it would bring forward a rise in US interest rates. It followed that, if investors could successfully predict employment, they could forecast the dollar. For most months in 1992-3 that would have worked, but not every month. Sometimes a weak employment report strengthened the dollar. And in 1994 the model changed, with a strong employment report indicating higher inflation and potential failure for Fed policy and therefore a weak dollar.

Many investors use charts to forecast exchange rates. Although chartists are all looking at the same picture they often come up with different predictions. Still, if enough people believe that, for example, a move below DM 1.45 means that the dollar will test DM 1.40, (a typical chartist prediction) then it could quickly become a self-fulfilling prediction.

Most investment managers take a longer term view, ignoring the day-to-day fluctuations of the markets. This still requires forecasting trends in the economy but arguably can give a better perspective. Others treat currency movements as a variable to be avoided and use hedging techniques including futures and options to eliminate or reduce their exposure.

Three key concepts

Before looking at the various forecasting approaches there are three important concepts that are useful to understand: "covered interest parity", "real exchange rates" (and the related concept, "real effective exchange rates") and the relationship between the current account and the capital account of the balance of payments.

Covered interest parity

This concept simply states that the difference between the forward exchange rate and the spot exchange rate is always equal to the difference between the interest rate in the two countries over the same period. If it were not then investors could quickly make money by borrowing in one currency, converting into another and entering into a forward contract to the first currency. It means of course that the currency with the higher interest rate will have a forward rate below its spot rate (and vice versa).

Sometimes the difference in interest rates is referred to as the "cost of hedging" though, strictly speaking this is incorrect. For example the US dollar based investor who decides to buy some Australian dollar bonds may choose to hedge the currency so that he is not exposed to the risk that the Australian dollar falls. But if Australian dollar one-year interest rates are one percent above US rates our investor will immediately lock in a 1% "loss" over a year since the forward exchange rate for Australian dollars will buy one percent less US dollars than the spot rate. The reason that this is not strictly a cost is that a one percent decline in the Australian dollar is the markets' best expectation and that expectation will also be factored into the yield on Australian bonds.

Real exchange rate

The concept of the real exchange rate is linked to the purchasing power parity (PPP) theory discussed below. As with other "real" concepts in economics the idea is to take inflation out of the equation. Real exchange rates are quoted as index numbers. For example taking the dollar/DM rate to be 100 on January 1st 1990, the movement since then in nominal terms has taken the dollar down (say) 10%, which would be measured as 90 on this index. The dollar has apparently become more competitive. But suppose that inflation in the US had been higher each year, say 3% p.a. higher, adding up to a cumulative 15%, then the real exchange rate index would be approximately 105, showing the US dollar to be less competitive. In effect the 15% higher price level has not been sufficiently compensated by the 10% devaluation.

The "real effective exchange rate" is the same idea, except that instead of being simply calculated between two countries it takes all the countries with which the country trades and weights them according to the size of trade. This is a concept to which the central banks pay particular attention in setting monetary policy. It is the best way to determine whether the exchange rate overall is depreciating in real terms (i.e. becoming more competitive), which would be a stimulus to the economy, or appreciating, which would be a contractionary force.

Forecasting Approaches

There are two broad approaches to forecasting exchange rates, though most forecasters probably use a combination of both. These are 1) approaches based on identifying some sort of fundamental or equilibrium exchange rate, and 2) approaches based on the relative strength of different economies, which will be evidenced in different interest rates, or different trends in monetary growth.

1. Fundamental or equilibrium exchange rates

The oldest theory of what determines exchanges rates is the so-called "purchasing power parity" theory. This theory is rooted in the idea that exchange rates are basically changing to keep trade in balance. Suppose for a moment that there was no international investment flow and that the only currency transactions were US importers buying (say) yen to pay their suppliers in Japan and US exporters changing their yen earnings back to dollars.

Then, if prices in Japan rose faster than in the United States, Japanese imports would not be able to compete so well in the US market and volumes would likely fall. At the same time US exports would rise because US products would have become more competitive. This would mean less demand for yen and more for dollars so that the dollar would rise.

On this view then, the exchange rate should change to keep different countries broadly competitive with each other. If it did not change then trade surpluses and deficits would become large, which cannot occur in the absence of capital flows to finance them. Another way of looking at it, is that exchange rates will tend to move to keep the purchasing power of the same amount of money constant. Thus if inflation is rising faster in the US than in Japan, the US dollar would be expected to depreciate over time.

There are a number of problems with this theory. *Firstly,* we know that, in practice, the size of currency transactions far outweighs the size of world trade. Total *daily* foreign exchange transactions in just the three largest markets, London, New York and Tokyo, amount to around $1,000 billion or $1 trillion, when world trade in a whole year amounts to about $5.3 trillion. *Secondly*, since there are increasingly large investment flows we know that large trade deficits can be financed for long periods so there is no reason for the exchange rate to adjust quickly. *Thirdly*, experience shows that exchange rates do indeed move very substantially over time, and far more than price trends would suggest. *Finally*, there are serious practical problems with estimating the PPP.

Calculating purchasing power parity

There are three approaches to calculating purchasing power parity though each inevitably contains a considerable margin of error. One is to try to directly compare goods prices in different countries. Note that the goods to be compared should be so-called "tradeable goods" since there is no reason why the price of a haircut or a MacDonalds hamburger should be the same in two different countries. Of the price you pay for a MacDonalds hamburger only a small proportion is actually a traded good, i.e. beef or wheat or tomatoes, the rest is "non-tradeable", e.g. transport costs, restaurant space or unskilled labour.

The second approach to measuring purchasing power parity, which is the one more commonly used, is to take a long period of 20 years or more and work out the average real exchange rate (i.e. adjust the exchange rate for relative inflation in the two countries) and work out what the average level has been. Then provided that the PPP theory works over the long term, that real level must be the PPP.

This approach faces a problem over which price index to use. For example to use the consumer price index would be to include a large number of goods and services prices which are not traded. To use the export price index would be to look at goods that are actually exported and not necessarily things that *might* have been exported at a different exchange rate. More commonly economists use the wholesale price index, as in the chart, but again this might not be a true reflection of tradeables prices.

Furthermore no price index fully accounts for changes in quality. For example most PPP calculations for the Yen come up with a figure in the area of Y120-150. Today's exchange rate is much stronger than that and yet Japan still enjoys a large

DM/Dollar: Actual and PPP

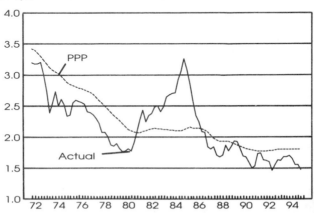

trade surplus with the United States. The reason is that the PPP calculation needs to take into account the improved competitiveness of Japanese industry throughout the 1980s by producing higher quality goods.

The third approach is fairly similar except, rather than taking the equilibrium exchange rate to be an average over a long period, the analyst picks one year when the exchange rate looked to be in equilibrium judging by the current account being in balance and then looks at relative inflation since then. So, if the US dollar/DM was in equilibrium in 1982 we can deduce what the equilibrium is now by allowing for the difference in inflation since then.

With all these methods in use and different price indices being employed, it is not surprising that estimates of PPP vary quite often by as much as 10 or 20%. Realistically therefore we can only estimate the PPP within a wide range. For example most economists would agree that the Deutschemark/ Dollar PPP is between DM 1.70 - 2.00, and the Yen/ Dollar 110 -140.

Finally, it should be noted that there may be reasons why a country should not be exactly in current account balance and therefore the equilibrium rate for the currency is not simply going to be the one that balances trade. For example it is often argued that developing countries are "natural" capital importers (i.e. run a current account deficit) because they have faster economic growth and high returns on investment. Equally the United States may have a natural tendency to "import" capital in a different sense, that foreigners simply want to hold dollars because it is the world's major currency for both transactions and investment. It makes no difference whether this inflow into dollars is from central banks wanting to buy US Treasury bills to hold in their foreign exchange reserves or whether it is ordinary people in Latin America or Eastern Europe preferring to hold dollar bills rather than the local currency. More than 50% of the US money stock, dollar bills, is believed to be held outside the United States.

Why PPP is still relevant

Hardly anyone believes that PPP is a useful guide to the direction of exchange rates in the short or even medium run. But it is still important for several reasons. *Firstly*, in broad terms it does seem to work in the very long run, meaning 5 years or longer. This is important for investors taking a long term position. *Secondly*, governments and central banks do take PPP very seriously in their approach to exchange rates. This is because they know that periods of under or over valuation may lead to sudden currency instability or be destabilising for business.

Thirdly, calculations of PPP are often a key factor in considerations by both governments and markets as to whether a particular fixed (or controlled) exchange rate can survive. For example most analysts argued (and the Bundesbank seemed to agree) that when Sterling entered the European Exchange Rate Mechanism the central rate chosen, DM 2.95, was too high. This view contributed to the strength of the speculation against the pound and may also have been behind the Bundesbank's unwillingness to help defend it.

Finally, there are times when PPP factors do seem to matter to the markets and dominate other factors. This usually happens when a large current account deficit is opening up and the markets question whether a growing deficit can be financed.

The Yen and PPP: why Tokyo is so expensive

Visitors to Tokyo often find living so expensive that they conclude that the yen must be massively overvalued on any kind of PPP comparison. Some attempts to calculate PPP come up with a level of 140 or weaker. Yet Japan has enjoyed a current account surplus for several years despite a much stronger currency.

The answer to this paradox is that Japan is very efficient at making so-called tradeable goods but generally very inefficient in many non-tradeable areas. For example, in areas such as cars and electronics, Japanese companies are extraordinarily efficient producing very high quality items at low cost. But much of Japan's service sector, including distribution networks and shops are highly inefficient by US standards and also face the high costs arising from shortage of space in a crowded country.

2. Relative economic strength

This approach focuses on currencies from the point of view of investment flows rather than trade flows. It says that currencies strengthen if their interest rates move up relative to other countries because investors switch into that currency to obtain the higher yield. This works best if the economy has plenty of spare capacity and therefore there is no immediate inflation threat. News of a rise in official interest rates will probably have the same effect though not if the markets judge that this rise will actually slow the economy and may soon be reversed.

Which interest rate is the most relevant? The answer is probably that both short and long term rates matter but bond yields are the most important. It is the bond market which is really telling us more about the state of the economy and therefore the likely direction of interest rates beyond the immediate term.

Combining PPP with relative strength

The relative strength approach tells us the response to news on the economy but does not tell us anything about the *level* of exchange rates. The PPP approach indicates what level of the exchange rate can be regarded as a long-term equilibrium. These two can be combined to generate a complete theory.

When interest rates are high in one country a flow of capital moves into that country, tending to raise the exchange rate. Even if investors begin to see the exchange rate as overvalued in some long term sense, they may still be content if they feel the extra yield compensates for that. However, once the exchange rate reaches an excessive level, they will question whether the high yield is enough to justify the likely exchange rate depreciation.

For example in 1985 investors were content with a DM/$ exchange rate in excess of DM3 because yields on bonds in the United States were around 4% p.a. higher than in Germany. Even given the likelihood that inflation would be higher in the United States, investors still enjoyed a real yield pick up of 2-3% in US bond yields compared with German bond yields. This would be enough to justify a 20-30% overvaluation.

What of the role of short rates? There is little question that short term interest rates can influence exchange rates but primarily in the short term. The level of short term interest rates influences the extent to which speculators are willing to bet against a currency. However the experience with fixed exchange rate systems *(see below)* suggests that short term interest rates can only have a temporary impact.

Government Intervention

Since 1971 the major world currencies have been floating against each other, although with varied degrees of government intervention to try to stabilise exchange rates. This followed the period in the 1950s and 1960s of fixed exchange rates. The Bretton Woods system eventually proved impossible to sustain as the US dollar became increasingly overvalued when US inflation picked up. The key advantage for governments of floating exchange rates is the avoidance of the humiliation of forced devaluations and the ability for the exchange rate to adjust to different inflation levels without major convulsions.

However the experience of floating exchange rates has not been as successful as many people expected in 1971 and there have been substantial moves to intervene in exchange rates. The two most important attempts to control exchange rates, from the investor's standpoint are G7 intervention to stabilise the major currencies and European activity in the form of the Exchange Rate Mechanism to stabilise exchange rates within Europe.

Does G7 intervention work?

Since the Plaza Agreement in 1985, the G7 finance ministers have met regularly to discuss economic coordination and have maintained target ranges for the major currencies, though the exact ranges have deliberately not been announced. There have also been numerous interventions to try to prevent exchange rates moving in a particular direction. The usual approach is to buy the weak currency in the spot market, making as much noise about it as possible. Such interventions can be and have been on a large scale though they will inevitably be dwarfed by the potential size of private capital movements.

Intervention therefore only works if it can persuade private investors that the currency will be held. This depends on a number of factors. Sometimes, especially if investors are already not sure how much further the currency can fall, government intervention can be enough to stop the move fairly easily. Obviously a great deal depends on the credibility of government intervention at that particular time.

In the middle 1980s the markets regarded central bank intervention with scepticism. Often it was treated as a chance to make money. By the end of the decade, though, intervention was being treated with much more respect. The authorities had learnt to use some clever tricks (or perhaps relearnt, since many of these tricks were used extensively in the 1970s). The "bear squeeze" for example, where speculators are lured into a trap and then very heavy intervention deliberately pushes the exchange rate a long way very quickly so that many speculators are forced to close out with a loss. Perhaps the most important technique, which has been used very extensively, is closely coordinated intervention. On occasion a dozen or more central banks would intervene together within the space of a few minutes.

Exchange rate theory suggests that if governments intervene in the FX market but do not allow interest rates to move to support the intervention, then they are likely to be unsuccessful. However the evidence since 1985 suggests that governments can create a view in the markets of where the exchange rate might go in the long term even if the market takes the exchange rate outside that range in the short term. Hence G7 actions may act to reinforce the idea of a fundamental exchange rate (or PPP) to which it must return in the long run. This is not altogether surprising since the G7 countries rely on sophisticated versions of purchasing power parity as their main indicator.

The European Exchange Rate Mechanism

Set up in 1979 the ERM was designed to enable European currencies to move within narrow ranges over periods of months or years while allowing periodic adjustments when inflation or trade pressures dictated. During the latter part of the 1980s it evolved into a more or less fixed exchange rate mechanism. By avoiding realignments governments hoped to convince the markets that they would not change over the long term and therefore to enable interest rates to come closer to German interest rates. Meanwhile other countries, which could not hope to avoid devaluation in the long run, including Spain, Italy and the UK were keen to use the exchange rate mechanism as an anchor to bringing down inflation. In that they were successful, until 1992.

The key point about the ERM is that it is a system for pegging to the Deutschemark. The Bundesbank is left in complete control of monetary policy and naturally determines it according to German needs. This is of course the main reason why France and some of the other "core" countries of the ERM are anxious to move to a full monetary union. Then a European central bank composed of representatives would vote on monetary policy according to conditions in all the member countries. If monetary union had existed in the early 1990s European short term interest rates would have been much lower and a general recession might have been avoided.

Is EMU feasible?

The Maastricht Treaty maps out a programme for monetary union in Europe by the end of the decade. This encouraged a major convergence in European bond yields during 1991 as the markets began to anticipate a single currency. After the collapse of the ERM in 1992-3 the markets reversed much of this move and are no longer focusing on EMU. But with the Intergovernmental Conference approaching in 1996, EMU is once again looking like a possibility at least for a core group of countries including France and Germany.

Ultimately whether this occurs will be a political decision in each of the countries but the issues are essentially threefold. *Firstly*, has there been sufficient convergence of inflation and interest rates and budget positions such that it would be easy to go to a single currency? The Maastricht Treaty laid down conditions for all three which at the time of writing would be fulfilled by very few countries and which will be very difficult to achieve even by the year 2000. However it is unlikely that strict fulfilment of the conditions would prevent monetary union if governments wanted it badly enough.

Secondly, is the integration of European economies sufficiently far advanced that it is sensible to have a single currency among different countries? In 1990-1 when the German unification allowed Germany and Holland to boom, the UK went into recession, suggesting that the economies were far from integrated. However with the 1992 process still leading to more reductions of barriers within Europe, the gradual move to a single economy is progressing. The issue here can be seen as whether better to achieve the single economic area first then go for a single currency or whether by going quickly to a single currency, the unified onomic area can be achieved more quickly.

The *final* question is the political one of whether governments are willing to give up their national currency and their national monetary sovereignty in order to have a single currency. Popular resistance to the loss of their own currency may be considerable and may well have been underestimated thus far, while the control of monetary policy by a single European central bank will substantially reduce the effective sovereignty of individual governments. There is little question that it is a major step on the road to European union and some countries at least may not be ready for this so soon.

Conclusion: exchange rates and investors

The analysis suggests several guidelines for dealing with currencies, though these are not hard and fast rules. *Firstly*, given the difficulty of currency forecasting the investor would be wise to be modest and to invest cautiously. *Secondly*, do not assume that because currencies have been responding in a particular way to particular news, that they will continue indefinitely to do so. *Thirdly*, be wary of government attempts to support over-valued exchange rates. They may succeed for a time, sometimes a long time, but nearly always eventually fail. *Fourthly*, expect G7 government intervention aimed at supporting weak currencies or selling strong currencies often to succeed.

10. Bond Markets

Two Approaches to Analysing Yields

Expectations of future short rates
Real yield plus inflation expectations

Economic Trends and Bonds

Bonds and economic growth
Bonds and inflation

Economic Policy and Bonds

Bonds and monetary policy
The yield curve
Bonds and fiscal policy
Judging the soundness of fiscal policy
Why does a high debt matter?

Bonds and the Cycle

Bonds in an International Context

Conclusion: bond markets and the investor

Bonds: Key concept

Price is inversely related to yield: Imagine a new 10 year bond successfully sold to the market at $100, which will pay $100 on maturity and $10 each year (the coupon) until then. We can say that the yield is 10%. Now suppose interest rates fall and the next 10 year bond issue (also issued at $100 and paying $100 on maturity) can be sold paying a coupon of only $8 each year. We can then say that long term interest rates or bond yields have fallen to 8%. The first bond issued, still paying $10 p.a. will be worth more than $100 now since it gives the holder $10 p.a. in income rather than $8. In fact its price will rise so that it too is yielding 8%.

Government bond markets are driven by economic trends, especially the pace of GDP growth and inflation, changes in monetary po and changes in fiscal policy. Bond prices genera. rise (i.e. yields fall) on news of slower economic growth, lower inflation and tighter fiscal policy. The effect of changes in monetary policy on bond yields depends on the markets' assessment of the impact on the economy. Sometimes a rise in short term interest rates can be good news for bonds, though usually not. Other bonds, from municipal bonds through to corporate bonds and junk bonds, follow a similar path to government bonds but with greater credit risk. Remember that when bond yields go down, the price of a bond rises and vice-versa (see box opposite).

This chapter is primarily about government bond yields where economics plays a crucial role. In most industrial countries governments are seen as the best credit risk, ultimately because they have the power both to raise taxes and to print money. However, as we shall see, many governments have allowed debts to rise rapidly in recent years and some among them, notably Italy, Sweden and Canada are now viewed with concern by investors.

The term "bond" is used here to describe any security (other than a short term Bill) of the "fixed income" variety, that is it promises a regular coupon payment, fixed at issue, plus a repayment at maturity. Other types of bonds such as floating rate notes (where the coupon payment varies with interest rates) or convertible bonds (providing an option to convert into a share) behave differently. Bonds with a fixed coupon lose value if market interest rates (for the same maturity) rise above the coupon, measured as a percent of the principal value. The longer the term of the bond the more sensitive its price to changes in interest rates. There are two distinct ways of looking at the yield on a bond.

ctations of future short rates

he approach is to treat the yield as an average of expected future interest rates plus some sort of risk premium. Consider a two year Treasury instrument for simplicity. Its yield can be viewed as an average of the current 3 month Treasury Bill rate and expectations of where 3 month rates will be over the following 21 months. There should also be a small premium for what is called the horizon risk, essentially the fact that the investor who buys this security is committing himself now.

If short term interest rates are expected to rise, the yield curve will be relatively steep with two year yields significantly above today's 3 month Treasury Bill rates. Sometimes though, when short term rates are particularly high because the central bank is trying to slow the economy to control inflation, the markets will anticipate that interest rates will come down so that two year bond yields will be below 3 months' rates.

Real yield plus inflation expectations

The second way of looking at bond yields is to break down the yield into two components, the so-called real bond yield and an estimate of inflation expectations. This enables the investor to take a view on whether bonds are cheap or expensive according to his view on whether the markets are too optimistic or too pessimistic on real yields and inflation.

In a few countries, for example the UK, Australia and Canada, a real yield exists in the market in the form of an indexed bond. These instruments pay a fixed coupon plus an adjustment for the rise in the consumer price index. In principle this allows us to compare the yield of these indexed bonds with the yield on similar dated ordinary bonds to give an ide of expected inflation. In practice tax effects probably distort the yields somewhat.

UK: Yield on Indexed Gilts

Source: DATASTREAM

For most countries, however, distinguishing the real yield from inflation expectations is a matter of judgement, arrived at by guessing at what the markets expect for inflation. Sometimes analysts use the latest inflation rate for this purpose but that is obviously flawed since very often the markets anticipate lower or higher inflation than current levels. Another alternative is to use forecasts of inflation but usually these do not go out beyond one or two years and yet bond buyers must consider up to a 10 year horizon or longer.

The expected inflation component of a bond yield can be further divided into expectations of inflation and a risk premium against those expectations being too optimistic. Suppose investors anticipate US inflation will average 3.5% p.a. over the long term. They may still require a risk premium of say ½% or 1% (the problem is that we do not know exactly what) to compensate for the possibility that inflation could be higher.

The two components of bond yields, the real part the inflation expectations, vary according to mic developments. So do short term interest

, which are determined by central banks and
ectations for short-term rates, which are
ermined by markets. The analysis below looks at
elds in relation to economic growth, inflation,
monetary policy, fiscal policy, and the economic
cycle.

Economic Trends and Bonds

Bonds and economic growth

News of faster economic growth generally depresses
bond prices, i.e. raises bond yields. This can be seen
as reflecting a change in expectations for short term
rates in the future: the markets expect that the
government will raise short term interest rates to
combat inflation. Alternatively using the second
approach above stronger growth can be seen as
working partly through expectations of higher
inflation and partly through higher real interest rates
because of an increase in demand for funds as
businesses and consumers borrow more.

Faster economic growth usually also means that the
government budget deficit will be smaller because of
improved tax revenues and lower unemployment
benefit payments. But although this means less bond
issuance and therefore should help bonds, the effect
is usually outweighed by the negative factors. The
reason for this is that the level of bond yields is not
just a price at which the market will accept this
year's new issuance, but a price that the market
demands for holding the whole accumulated stock of
debt.

Bonds and inflation

News of higher inflation is bad for bonds. If the
economy is growing fast and especially if it is close
to full employment and full capacity, then the
markets will be expecting a rise in inflation at some
point. If inflation is slow to pick up, as it was in the
United States in 1994 for example, the bond marke
will be relieved but are unlikely to rally strongly
long as the economy stays strong.

Of course for long term bonds the inflation rat
the next year or two is only part of the problem
since the investor is taking a bet over 10 years or
more. The markets have to take a view on where
governments and central banks will allow inflation
to go in the long run.

USA: 30 Year Yields and Inflation

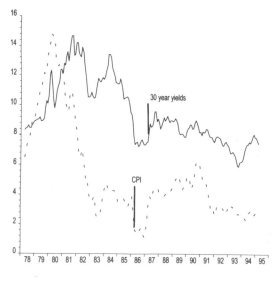

Source: DATASTREAM

In the 1970s bond market investors lost out heavily
because they failed to appreciate that the authorities
would, in the interests of employment and short
term economic growth, allow a major inflation to
develop from the rise in oil prices. Between 1972
and 1982 inflation averaged 8.7% p.a. in the USA,
14.1% in the UK and 5.1% in Germany. Bond yields
lagged behind inflation for much of the decade,
especially in the UK and the USA.

Around 1980, led by the Federal Reserve chairman
Paul Volcker and Mrs Thatcher's new Conservative
government in the UK an altogether tougher
approach to inflation appeared. Between 1982 and
1992 inflation was held to an average 3.8% p.a. in
USA, 5.4% in the UK and 2.2% in Germany.

people believe that the new aversion to
on is here to stay and that the central banks

allow inflation to return to the levels seen in
70s. In recent years central banks have been
more independence in monetary policy. At the
the time central bankers themselves have become
ronger in their belief that keeping inflation low is
the central objective of monetary policy, and indeed,
for many, the only objective. There is general
consensus that 2% inflation is the ideal, although
some central banks seem to regard 2% as a long term
target average and others see it more as a floor. For
the latter group, which probably includes the
Federal Reserve, the ceiling for inflation, beyond
which draconian monetary tightening should be
expected, may now be around 4% p.a.

Still, for the long term investor, the question is
whether this new aversion to inflation will really
last. Faced with prolonged slow growth or high
unemployment or social unrest can governments and
central banks be relied upon not to stoke the
inflationary fires?

Economic Policy and Bonds

Bonds and monetary policy

A hike in short term interest rates has a number of
contradictory effects on bond investors' perceptions.
Firstly, it is liable to raise expectations of the future
level of short term interest rates because it implies
that the authorities are concerned about the outlook
for inflation. This usually means that the front end of
the yield curve at least (say out to 3 years) will rise.

Secondly, using the other model of what
determines bond yields, a rise in short rates may
increase the real interest rate component of a bond
yield. If the markets expect that the central bank will
keep short term interest rates above the rate of
inflation (which did not always happen in the 1970s
but is now a key part of central bank orthodoxy),
then the real rate on bonds will rise or otherwise
investors might just as well hold deposits and simp
roll them over.

Thirdly, the effect on inflation expectations is

ambiguous. If the rise in short term rates is seen strong move by the central bank, which is likely slow the economy and therefore improve the inflation outlook, then bonds will rally. But if the rise in short rates is not thought to be large enough to slow the economy, then inflation expectations could rise.

The yield curve

The yield curve is a chart of the whole range of yields at different maturities. A so-called "normal" yield curve shows rising yields for longer term bonds. The reason is that, in order to be prepared to buy longer term bonds, investors need a premium over shorter term bonds, sometimes called the "horizon" premium or the "bond maturity" premium. The exact slope varies during the economic cycle as discussed below and also depends on long term expectations for growth and inflation.

The shape of the yield curve is one of the most useful ways to determine both the status of monetary policy and the stage of the cycle. When it is inverted strongly then monetary policy is particularly tight. The fact that bond yields are much lower than short rates is saying that the markets expect the level of interest rates to slow the economy in time, allowing interest rates to come down. When the curve is particularly steeply upward sloping, with short term interest rates well below long term interest rates, this is likely to be a sign of monetary ease (most often seen during recessions or the early stages of recovery). The central bank is trying to boost the economy and the bond markets are concerned that interest rates will have to rise soon.

Bonds and fiscal policy

onds are issued by governments to finance budget
cits and the relationship between bond yields
government fiscal policy is very important.
ally speaking we would expect that if

...ments issue more bonds, because public ...ces are showing a larger deficit, then they will ...e to offer investors a higher yield to take on those ...nds. In other words a large fiscal deficit should be ...ssociated with higher bond yields.

However the fact that governments borrow more one year than the previous year does not change the stock of government debt outstanding by very much. Moreover government deficits tend to be highest just when other borrowings are lowest. Deficits are typically large at a time of recession when tax receipts are down and payments for unemployment benefit, etc. are higher. But it is at just this time that business investment is weak and savings are high (because consumers are saving for fear of unemployment). Hence there may actually be strong demand for government paper.

Also, quite often in recessions, short term interest rates are low and the yield curve is steeply upward sloping. This makes holding bonds relatively attractive compared with deposits or Treasury Bills, because the central bank is trying to generate recovery. In the recession in the early 1990s, a substantial part of bond issuance was taken up by banks, taking advantage of the steeply upward sloping yield curve. Hence, in a cyclical time frame, it is not clear that a rising budget deficit leads to higher bond yields.

However it does seem clear that bond yields are influenced by long-run expectations of whether the government is running a sound fiscal policy or not. An unsound fiscal policy may raise the possibility of default in the extreme case. More commonly the worry is over the pace of growth of outstanding debt and the possibility of higher inflation.

Judging the soundness of fiscal policy

In considering whether or not fiscal policy is sound, the best analytical approach is to look at the level of government debt and its trend direction. The maximum ratio of government debt to GDP laid down in the Maastricht Treaty for economic and monetary union in Europe was 60%. This is an arbitrary number but is probably a reasonable leve to consider as the limit to prudence.

Consider the case of a country with a ratio of debt to GDP of 100% (for example Italy or Belgium, though these countries are somewhat above 100%). If the budget deficit is 10% of GDP, then total debt will rise by 10% that year. Unless GDP itself, including both the real component and inflation, rises by more than 10% then the debt ratio will rise. For example if inflation is 3% and growth 2% then GDP will rise by only 5% and in one year's time the debt ratio will be approximately 105% of GDP (110 divided by 105).

It is easy to deduce that a sound fiscal policy from this high level of debt requires that the deficit as a per cent of GDP must be less than GDP growth (including inflation). For example if the deficit is 2% while nominal GDP rises 5% then the debt ratio will fall to approximately 97% (102 divided by 105). Note the temptation here for governments to use higher inflation to control the ratio.

For countries with high debt, lower interest rates are an important factor in reducing the budget deficit. If the average interest rate paid by the government on its debt drops from 10% to 8% then the budget deficit itself, even without any reduction in other expenditures or increases in taxation, will drop to 8% too. This makes it possible for countries to set up a virtuous circle. If expenditure can be cut and taxes raised then not only will the deficit before interest payments (known as the primary balance) fall but interest rates are likely to fall too because of the slowdown in the economy which will add to the decline in the budget deficit. A downside to this situation is that GDP growth may also be weaker as the real component declines and inflation declines too. In practice reducing a debt ratio of 100% down to a healthy level like 50% is likely to take 10 years or more.

ost countries have a ratio of debt to GDP of nearer and here the arithmetic for controlling the ratio out rather differently. Consider a country

...e the budget deficit is 10% of GDP and GDP is ...ng 5%. At the end of the year debt will be at 60, ...ile GDP will be at 105, giving a new ratio of 57%. ...n this case, keeping the deficit to GDP ratio the same as the growth rate of nominal GDP, is not good enough. Debt would be at 55 and GDP at 105 which is equal to a rise in the debt ratio to 52.4%. In fact to keep the debt ratio at 50% the ratio of the budget deficit to GDP must be no more than half the rate of growth of nominal GDP. It was this arithmetic which made debt ratios rise sharply in both Europe and the United States in the early 1990s.

Why does a high debt matter?

A rapid rise in debt worries the markets because then governments may find it more and more difficult to manage the public finances. In the extreme case bond-holders start to fear that the government will either default (wholly or partially) or deliberately push up the rate of inflation so that the real value of outstanding bonds dwindles.

There is no single level at which the debt ratio becomes critical but beyond 100% the pressure to reduce it becomes more and more substantial, leaving governments with very few options. Bond markets then have to worry whether the government has the political strength to push through the inevitable tax rises and spending cuts which are implied.

In the next century most countries face a serious problem from ageing populations. Commitments to paying state pensions (notably in Continental Europe) and to meeting rising demands on health care (particularly in the United States) mean that, as the population of retired people increases in the next 20-30 years, the demands on government spending will rise substantially.

The ageing problem is dramatically illustrated by the example of Japan. In Japan the figure for net de' to GDP is just above zero, the lowest among the major countries. Yet the Ministry of Finance was' very reluctant to use expansionary fiscal policy'

pull Japan out of recession in 1993-94. The Minis
of Finance argues that it is more appropriate to loc
at the gross debt figure in Japan. The main differenc
between the two is the accumulated reserves of the
social security fund which have been invested in
government bonds. But beginning around the turn of
the century, the social security fund will move into
deficit, and these bonds will have to be sold. So,
taking this long-term view, the Japanese government
is quite right when it argues that its debt position is
much worse than the net debt figure would suggest.

Bonds and the Cycle

All the linkages discussed above play a role in the
behaviour of bonds during the cycle. In the *recovery*
phase of the cycle, inflation is likely to be low and
falling and short term interest rates are still low as
the central bank is trying to encourage recovery.
Bond yields tend to fall (prices rise), helped by low
inflation expectations and low real rates. The yield
curve is normally upward sloping.

During the *early upswing* phase of the cycle, bond
yields are stable or might start to edge up as the
market anticipates higher inflation down the road
and real rates rise with increased borrowing in the
economy. Also the authorities may be beginning to
nudge up short term interest rates.

During the *late upswing* phase of the cycle,
inflation is rising and the central bank is pushing up
interest rates to try to cool the economy down. Real
rates too are often high because borrowing reaches a
peak. Bond yields will rise but how much depends
on how overheated the economy has become and
how quickly the markets expect the central bank to
slow the economy.

In the fourth stage of the cycle where the *economy
slows* or goes into recession, bond yields are likely to
peak and come down. The key point is that, with the
economy going into recession, there will be hopes of
er inflation and therefore the expected inflation
ponent should be coming down. At the same
a weaker economy points to lower demands on

s (lower real rates) and also lower short term
rest rates as time goes forward. Bond yields will
arly always begin to fall before short term interest
ates. However, in this phase, because the yield
curve is typically inverted, with short term interest
rates above bond yields, bond yields may still be
constrained from declining. The problem is that
banks or other institutions holding bonds, though
they may be looking forward to capital gains, will
have to fund those bonds at a loss through the higher
short term interest rates.

The final stage of the cycle, *recession*, is usually the
best period for bond markets. The prospect of lower
inflation and lower interest rates means that bond
yields will be coming down. At this stage though, the
bond markets will be all the time wondering how
soon the recovery will come and how low they can
expect inflation to fall.

This view of the cycle may appear to offer an easy
way to make money. The problems are that it is
always uncertain as to how long each phase will last
and how intense it will be. The markets will already
have factored in all the existing news on the state of
the cycle. For example during the early stages of the
upswing, it is entirely uncertain as to whether the
upswing will in fact last several years, eventually
bringing severe overheating and high inflation. Or
whether it will be a short upswing with inflation not
rising much.

Similarly during the recession stage it is very hard
to know whether the recovery will happen next
month or in two years' time. If it occurs next month,
then the low for inflation is only a year or so away. If
the recovery itself is still a year off, then inflation
will be likely to fall for another year and not reach its
low for more than two years. Bond yields can fall
further.

In 1994 bond markets suffered a severe crash
everywhere and yet, while the US economy was
probably moving into the late upswing phase of the
cycle, Germany and Japan were only just entering
the recovery phase. This demonstrates the
uncertainty involved in trying to use analysis of

cycle to time entry into bonds. What seems to have happened in the US is that a normal two year bear market was telescoped into a few months. The simultaneous crash in Europe demonstrates the increasing internationalisation of the bond markets.

Bonds in an International Context

Bond yields in different countries are linked through exchange rates. If a country has a formal link with another country, for example, through the European Exchange Rate Mechanism or if the link is informal e.g. Canada with the US dollar, then the markets will look at the bond yield in relation to the exchange rate. Typically one country is seen as the strong currency country where the combination of good fiscal management and low inflation trends in the long run mean that currency is unlikely to depreciate against the other. Then the country pegging will need to offer bond holders a premium because of a risk of a devaluation in the long term. If a country can convince the market that its currency will not devalue, either because inflation is particularly low or if the currency has already fallen significantly, then bond yields could go under yields in the other country.

Conclusion: bond markets and the investor

There is a powerful school of thought, particularly in the UK but becoming stronger in the United States, that for long term capital growth, investment in equities is much better than investment in bonds. Certainly this has been the historical experience over long periods in the English speaking countries, though less so in Germany over the last 20 years and not so much so in the UK and the US in the last 5 years.

Bonds, especially shorter dated bonds, are attractive to investors investing for short periods who may need the money fairly soon. Volatility is lower than the stock markets and there is therefore less risk of a significant decline. Bonds are also

ave to hold as a proportion of a long term
al growth portfolio. They can help to even out
swings in equity portfolios, since at certain
ints in the cycle bond yields will do well while
tock markets do badly, notably in the early stages of
a recession. In that way they offer investors
diversification.

The best time to buy bonds, or in the context of an
overall portfolio to go overweight in bonds, is when
bond yields look high in relation to inflation and
there is a good chance of an economic slowdown. As
discussed above, timing is always difficult and there
are no hard and fast rules. Ultimately the key factor is
whether central banks are thought likely to be tough
on inflation.

11. Stock Markets

Factors Affecting Earnings

Long term influences on earnings
Cyclical factors affecting earnings

Impact of Interest Rates

Short rates
The impact of bond yields
Liquidity

Valuing Stock Markets

Price-earnings ratios
Price-cash earnings ratios
Dividend yield
Yield gap or ratio
Price-book value

Historical Performance of Equities

The equity premium

Emerging Markets

Conclusion: Stocks and the Investor

In general stock markets rise with economic growth, because of the consequent growth in company earnings. Recessions, higher interest ra. and political uncertainty are usually bad for markets. However, sometimes higher interest rates are taken as a good sign, indicating strong growth or a central bank that is in charge. Stocks tend to be more volatile than other asset classes such as bonds. Stock markets typically have one or two years in the economic cycle that show much of the rise for the cycle and one year with a major correction. The major rise often happens in the middle of the recession when the markets suddenly anticipate an upturn. The downturn often happens when valuations are stretched and the markets suddenly anticipate an economic slowdown or are upset by a political "shock". It would be wonderful if investors could time the market to miss the down-year but the risk is always that they will miss the good years!

While stock markets are ultimately made up of a host of individual companies, each with their own risks and potentialities, there is a tendency for many stock prices to move in the same direction over time. The focus of this chapter is the economic forces which move the market as a whole. These forces can be divided into two elements, the economic factors affecting company earnings and the impact of interest rates, both short term interest rates and long term bond yields.

Factors Affecting Earnings

Company earnings, or profits, are the key to stock prices. They provide dividends for investors and most of the finance for investment to boost the company's earnings in future. Many brokers make forecasts for company earnings to provide the basis r buy, hold or sell recommendations. Forecasts for nings for the market as a whole are sometimes l on aggregating these forecasts for all the ual stocks, the so-called "bottom up"

...h and sometimes based on an aggregate
..., incorporating forecasts for economic growth,
...tion and interest rates, etc., the "top down"
...proach.

Long term influences on earnings

It is useful to separate long term trend influences
from shorter term cyclical factors. Longer term trend
growth in company earnings is mainly determined
by the trend rate of growth of the economy. A faster
growing economy is likely to show faster average
earnings growth. This is one reason for the
popularity of emerging markets.

Another long term trend influence is the effect of a
liberalisation of economic policy on the growth of
profits. Economic liberalisation, a widespread trend
in many countries over the last decade, involves
measures such as reducing bureaucratic controls on
investment and bank lending, easing labour laws,
reducing tariffs, eliminating prohibitions on imports
and freeing prices. For some companies these
measures have the effect of reducing margins,
because of the increase in competition, both
domestic and foreign. But they also raise returns on
investment and often, also, allow companies to use a
longer term time horizon. The liberalisation trend
has been another reason for the popularity of
emerging markets in recent years.

A key long term factor is the behaviour of wages. In
countries where labour takes a high proportion of
companies' sales revenues, margins are low and
profits limited. This is sometimes a long-run problem
in countries where strong labour laws or powerful
trades unions prevent the expansion of profits. In the
UK for example, wages amounted to around 68% of
GDP in the 1970s but in the new environment of the
1980s, with higher unemployment and weakened
trades unions, the percentage fell to 64%.

Finally, among long term factors, the flexibility that
companies enjoy to respond to new circumstances
may be a key factor in long term earnings growth.
This flexibility probably comes mainly from easy
labour laws, which permit lay-offs or redundanc...

but it may also be a cultural issue. There has
much debate for example as to whether Japan
companies have as much flexibility as US comp
to deal with slower growth. The tradition of life-t
employment in Japan may militate against it and,
unlike the past, Japan may find it difficult to grow
out of trouble.

In the second half of the 1990s there is evidence
that international competition through trade
liberalisation and privatisation is forcing companies
everywhere to adopt a tough "compete or die"
philosophy, which is likely to bring rewards to the
successful but may also increase the risks for the
laggards.

Cyclical factors affecting earnings

Company earnings tend to go through a cycle in line
with the economic cycle. Years of rapid earnings
growth typically occur near the beginning of an
upswing while earnings usually fall in recession *(see
chart)*. Some companies, generally the ones with
large fixed costs and a pronounced sales cycle, are
more sensitive to the economic cycle than others and
these are called "cyclical stocks". Examples include
car manufacturers and chemicals producers.

During *recession*, earnings are depressed because
of reduced sales and margins and therefore lower
overall revenues to set against fixed costs. In severe
recessions earnings can disappear altogether for
these companies, while other companies less
affected by the cycle, for example food companies,
may see very little change in earnings.

In the *recovery* stage of the economic cycle
earnings are still low, though may be starting to grow
again. Both companies and the stock market hope
that the worst may be over. Interest rates are usually
low, which of course helps corporate cash flow and
may also allow an improvement in balance sheets
with longer term debt replacing short term debt.
'so companies have usually cut costs by this stage.
the *early upswing* phase earnings recover and
often show rapid growth rates. Remember that

% decline in earnings it takes a 100% rise in
s to come back to the starting point! Two
s probably lie behind much of this
ovement. One is the rise in capacity utilisation
industrial companies and the fuller use of staff by
l companies. Costs stay the same while volume
rises, sometimes margins too, which brings large
increases in profits. For the economy as whole this is
measured as an increase in productivity, i.e. output
per unit of input. At this stage of the cycle wage
awards usually remain modest because of continuing
relatively high unemployment so that most of the
gains flow straight into profits rather than increased
wages.

UK: Company Earnings

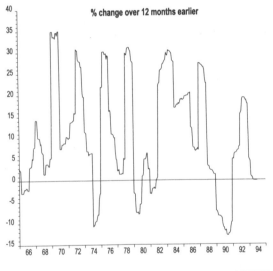

% change over 12 months earlier

Source: DATASTREAM

The second factor is often the efficiency gains made
during the recession which do not really show up
until output rises. Recessions tend to concentrate
managements' minds and provide extra discipline on
workers, because of the threat of job losses. The
result is that some of the "fat" built up during the
growth years, including both obvious waste and
"luxury" projects, are cut out. A leaner, fitter
company emerges from recession.

During the *late upswing* phase of the business cycle earnings typically do very well from high capacity use and rising margins. But they may be threatened by rising wages and higher interest rates. If inflation has picked up then companies gain from stock (inventory) appreciation. But earnings forecasts are likely to be better if inflation is slow to pick up because then the late phase of the business cycle will likely last longer.

The final stage of the economic cycle, as the *economy slows* and goes into recession, sees the beginning of an earnings decline. Capacity utilisation falls, raising unit costs. Usually wage growth is slow to adjust to the cycle and so eats further into company earnings. Lay-offs or redundancies may also be slow to come. Finally interest rates are often still high at this point, sometimes penally high, which also impacts earnings.

Impact of Interest Rates

The second broad impact of economic factors on the economy is the effect of interest rates and bond yields. As we saw above interest rates affect stocks by impacting on earnings. But more important is their effect by changing the relative attractiveness of stocks to other assets especially short term deposits and long term bond yields. Generally speaking a rise in short rates and/or bond yields is bad for stocks, but sometimes the effect may be outweighed by strong company earnings growth. Companies such as utilities and banks tend to be influenced strongly by interest rates and are known as "interest-sensitive" stocks.

Short rates

The effect on stocks of a rise in interest rates may depend on whether it represents a rise in real interest rates or a rise in inflation expectations. A ▓se in inflation expectations should mean that ▓ecasts of earnings growth are raised too so that ▓k prices are unmoved. However the experience the 1970s suggests that this is not always the case. The problem may be that when investors see higher inflation they begin to worry that the authorities will soon tighten policy bringing the economic upswing to an end. Or perhaps the rise in inflation causes investors to require a greater risk premium on stocks, which implies a fall in price.

USA: Interest Rates and Stocks

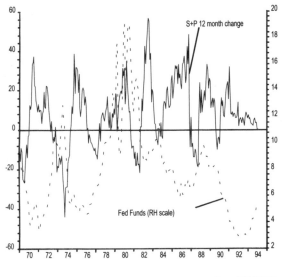

Source: DATASTREAM

A change in the real component of short term interest rates means that the monetary authorities have tightened economic policy. Not only does this make an economic slowdown more likely, which would impact on earnings but it makes holding deposits (or "cash") more attractive. This is not to say that stocks will automatically fall in price. The markets could conclude that the rise in interest rates is confirmation of the strong trend in economic growth. They might also decide that the rise in rates will control the economic upswing better and help to avoid an early downturn. But if the markets become convinced that the authorities are determined to end the upswing, to fight inflation then stocks will be weak.

In recent years, particularly in the US, the authorities have often spoken of their intention achieve a soft landing, rather than a full blown recession. In practice managing the economy to achieve this is very difficult because of the uncertainties and lags in policy. Nevertheless, if inflation has not picked up too much the markets may interpret a rise in interest rates as good news because of the chance of achieving that soft landing.

However, as short term interest rates rise they provide an increasingly high return investment alternative to stocks at a time when the risk of holding stocks looks to be increasing. In the 1970s, although stocks performed poorly, deposits were not a safe haven because interest rates were often less than the inflation rate. In the 1990s, with central banks more independent and vigilant against the threat of inflation, deposit rates tend to be above the inflation rate.

The impact of bond yields

A change in bond yields can also have a direct impact on stocks and one measure of the relative valuation of stocks and bonds compares bond yields with dividend yields *(see below)*. As with short rates, a rise in bond yields that is due to a rise in inflationary expectations should not affect stock prices in theory but in practice often does.

However a rise in the real component of bonds is more likely to be positive than a rise in the real component of short term interest rates. While it does increase the attractiveness of holding bonds rather than stocks it also implies that the economy is strong and earnings growth should be rapid. Hence a period of high real interest rates on bonds can be a good period for stocks too. The early 1980s was a good example.

An inverted yield curve, i.e. when short term rates higher than bond yields, might be expected to be for stocks but this has not always been the case. may be because it is generally a time of high

growth, though it may also reflect hopes of
...anding rather than a hard landing.

...uidity

There is plenty of historical evidence that rapid
money supply growth correlates with rising stock
markets. Many stock market analysts use measures of
liquidity, such as the growth in money supply minus
the rate of inflation to measure this effect. Rapid
growth in money supply is often associated with low
short term interest rates, because it means that the
cost of borrowing is low. For example the run-up in
US stocks in early 1987 or the boom in Japanese
stocks throughout 1986-9, or the rise in world stock
markets in 1993 can be linked to over-easy monetary
policy. However, liquidity can grow fast and stock
markets gain ground even with rising interest rates,
if confidence is high enough.

Valuing Stock Markets

A variety of different measures are used to value
stock markets with the five discussed below the most
common. These measures are best used to compare
current values with past historical values for the
same country. Using them to compare across
countries is more difficult because of different tax
treatment of company earnings and dividends as well
as other factors.

Price-earnings ratios

Perhaps the most common valuation measure, this is
the ratio of a stock price (or a market as a whole) to
its earnings and is widely quoted in the newspapers.
A high ratio may suggest that the market is expensive
while a low ratio suggests it is cheap. Sometimes this
ratio is expressed the other way around as an
earnings yield. For example a price-earnings ratio of
12 is equal to an earnings yield of 8.33%. Fast
growing companies or countries tend to have
relatively high price-earnings ratios and vice-ver

Japan has had extremely high price-earnings for many years, but it is impossible to compar directly with other countries. One reason is tha different treatment of company accounts means profits are kept lower than in the US. Another is th Japanese companies own each other through a complex web of cross-holdings. This has the effect of exaggerating the number of shares outstanding and therefore depressing earnings per share. For these and other reasons many analysts prefer to look at the ratio of price to cash earnings.

S=P 500: Price-Earnings Ratio

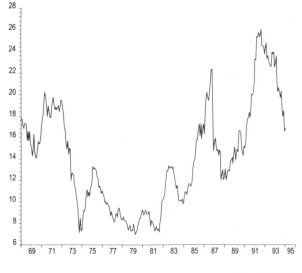

Source: DATASTREAM

Price-cash earnings ratios

The attraction of this ratio is that it measures cash earnings before depreciation which is treated differently in different countries. Japan, for example, has a price-cash earnings ratio much closer to the US on this measure. In the late 1980s when Japan's price-earnings ratio reached 70 or more at the peak the market, the price-cash earnings ratio was only d eight.

...easure is the ratio of dividends to stock prices. ...tionally the UK has a high ratio, due to high ...ation and the tax treatment of dividends while ...pan has a very low ratio, in recent years often less than 1%. In the UK and to some extent the US, maintenance of this ratio is taken very seriously, even when profits are down, so that the "pay out ratio", the proportion of earnings paid in dividends, can vary widely.

Yield gap or ratio

This is a comparison of the earnings or dividend yield on stocks with a long bond yield. Most commonly it is expressed as a ratio of the long bond yield to the dividend yield. But it can also be expressed as a difference between the two. Before the 1960s, in a time of low inflation, it was generally expected that the yield on equities would be higher than the yield on bonds to reflect the extra risk involved. But since then, due to higher inflation, bond yields have been higher than dividend yields, and usually higher than earnings yields, giving rise to the so-called "reverse yield gap".

Using this ratio is difficult because of its sensitivity to inflation. Only where the existence of index linked bonds provides a market for real bond yields, such as in the UK, can we be sure what the ratio means.

Price-book value

Another commonly used ratio, this one is particularly dangerous in cross-country comparisons but does give some indication of the stock's current valuation in relation to recent history. As the name suggests it takes the ratio of the price of a share to its book value. Perhaps in years to come the tax and accounting treatment of companies will be standardised across the world but, at the moment, law and practise vary widely.

Historical Performance of Equities

Most professional investors take the view that a
diversified portfolio of stocks is likely to be more
volatile but over the long term provide a better
return than either bonds or cash. This has generally
been the historical experience, notably in the US and
UK where data go back a long way, but also makes
sense theoretically, since stocks are likely to be more
risky than government bonds and therefore should
give investors a higher return.

However, there have been periods when superior
returns from stocks have taken a long time to come,
ten years or more, and in some countries the
historical record is less clear-cut than in the US and
UK. Extreme cases such as Russian equities from pre
1917 obviously show the risk of investing in any
country if the economic system changes.

The worst periods historically for stocks, were from
1929 into the early 1930s and the 1970s. Between
September 2nd 1929 and July 8th 1932 the US Dow
Jones index declined 89.2%, which is to say that it
fell to only just over 10% of its previous value!
Contrary to legend this was caused by a long bear
market rather than the 1929 Crash. On Black
Monday, October 28th 1929, the Dow did fall 12.8%,
but by the end of that week, despite falling again on
Tuesday, the market was only 8.5% below its level
the previous Friday. The long bear market was linked
to a catastrophic recession, or depression, which
saw US GDP fall by around 30%.

The second major episode of poor stock
performance was in the 1970s when a period of
relatively weak economic growth coincided with
unexpectedly high inflation caused by the
quadrupling of oil prices in late 1973.

In the 1930s, with the general price level falling,
investors would have been better off in deposits
(provided that the bank did not fail). In the 1970s
deposits and bonds were poor investments too,
because interest rates were often below the rate of
inflation. Inflation hedges such as property and
commodities were generally the best bet.

…0s was an extremely good period for … with market indices quadrupling or more … the decade. This bull market is explained by … main factors. *Firstly*, it reflected a rebound … the weakness at the start of the decade. This … due to the recession of that time and pessimism that, just as in the late 1970s, the recession would give way to a short-lived upswing.

Secondly, there was a sustained improvement in profit growth in many countries in the 1980s. This was due both to the strong economic upswing and, in some countries notably the UK, an increase in the share of profits in output. *Thirdly,* the fall in inflation itself meant that the quality of profits improved, with more being due to genuine margin and less arising simply from stock (inventory) appreciation.

In 1990 stocks were impacted by the recession in the English speaking countries and the uncertainties of the Gulf conflict. But since 1991 stock markets have performed well, with 1993 an excellent year but 1994 a weak year.

The equity premium

Equities are inherently more risky than bonds, especially government bonds. Governments can raise taxes to repay bonds while companies have to compete in the markets to make profits and, if they fail, equity investors are the last in the queue for any money after all the other creditors including bond-holders. For this reason investors are likely to demand a premium, i.e. an extra return, for holding stocks and this is known as the equity premium.

As described above, equities have indeed tended to provide higher returns than bonds but, strictly speaking, the equity premium refers to *expected* returns, not actual returns. In other words, the price of a stock, or a market, should be such that the investor looks like earning a higher return in stocks than in bonds. In practice, to calculate the equity premium requires assumptions about inflation and expectations of future dividend growth.

Most calculations suggest that the equity prer
on US stocks has been falling since the 1950s an
may now be down to around 2-3% compared with
7% in the past. One reason for this decline is that it
reflects the improved confidence in stocks now,
with the memories of the 1929-32 bear market
largely forgotten. Indeed the 1987 experience
seemed to confirm that it could be forgotten because
stock markets in 1988-9 recovered quickly from the
Crash. This view is reinforced by some historical
studies which suggest that the equity premium was
in the 2-3% range in the 19th century and right up to
1929. On this view the period from 1929 to the late
1950s was the unusual period.

Another argument though is that the relative risk of
stocks to bonds or deposits has been re-rated by
investors. The experience of the 1970s showed the
dangers of holding bonds and how the slightest
whiff of inflation sends bond yields skywards.
Meanwhile the ability of institutional investors and
mutual funds to diversify stock holdings means that
the risk of holding a stock portfolio can be reduced.

Emerging Markets

Emerging markets are defined by the International
Finance Corporation, IFC, (part of the World Bank)
as any stock market in a country with per capita
income less than $8356 in 1994. Obviously this
definition, like any other, is to some extent arbitrary.
Some poor countries have tiny stock markets which
have yet to emerge. Another, Hong Kong, is too rich
to be included as an emerging market, yet given its
legendary volatility and heavy reliance on China,
which is an emerging market, it probably should be.

Emerging markets have been increasingly popular
in recent years for several reasons. One is that many
countries have been opening up their economies and
markets to foreign investors. Another is that
ountries have been generating rapid economic
wth and therefore profits growth. Latin countries
shown good performance as well as Asian
ts.

reason for these markets' popularity among
ional investors is that they have tended to
relatively independently (i.e. a low correlation)
n the major markets. This means that they can
wer the risk of a portfolio. Finally, and this sounds
note of warning, investors' returns have often been
very good because valuations have risen. When
price-earnings ratios move up from the 10-15 range
to the 15-20 range, investors enjoy very good
returns. But these cannot be repeated unless
valuations rise still higher.

Two key characteristics of these markets stand out.
One is that in practice investment in stocks in these
markets can be difficult. Information is often
deficient, markets thin, often only a few stocks in
each market are really "investable" and settlement
slow. The other is that these markets usually show
much greater volatility than developed markets.

Conclusion: Stocks and the Investor

Experience and theory both suggest that, for long
term capital growth, stocks should form a substantial
part of an investor's portfolio. While most investors
would love to time the markets, for example
anticipating recessions and avoiding bear markets,
this is very difficult. Being out of the market is
almost as dangerous as being in it, because of the
possibility of missing a strong rally. Most
professional investors trim or add to their stock
portfolios only at the margin during the economic
cycle and concentrate more on individual stock
picking to add value.

12. Commodity Markets

Overview

Key Economic Influences

World growth
US inflation
US interest rates

Categories of Commodities

Precious metals
Fuels
Industrial raw materials
Foods and beverages

Long Run Trends in Commodity Prices

Commodity Indices

Commodities and the investor

Overview

For investors, commodities play the role of an inflation hedge. There is historical evidence that a small proportion of commodities or commodity company stocks in a diversified portfolio can lower the overall risk because commodity prices tend to move up when bonds and stocks are weak. But the view, widely held in the 1970s, that there would be increasing shortages of raw materials and therefore prices would show a long term uptrend, has been discredited. The prices of commodities are mainly determined by the supply and demand for each individual commodity. Seasonal factors, political upsets and labour disputes play a significant role as well as long term trends for that particular commodity. The key economic influences on commodities are world economic growth, US inflation and US interest rates. Generally, commodity prices rise with stronger growth, higher inflation and lower interest rates. Gold is seen as a hedge against inflation and political instability. Oil prices, which had such a major influence on the world economy in the 1970s, are now much less significant.

Key Economic Influences

World growth

Fast economic growth, especially when it is simultaneously fast in a number of countries, as in 1972-3 or 1994-5, means strong demand for commodities. This is especially likely if industries such as cars and house building are strong, because of their heavy use of raw materials such as copper and timber. Still, this will only have a strong impact on prices if stocks are low and commodity producers are near capacity. In 1972-3, after years of strong economic growth, many were, especially oil producers. The result was a massive upturn in commodity prices, led by oil, which lasted for nearly 0 years. In the 1980s commodity prices were generally weak as capacity developed in the 1970s came on stream. Prices rose in 1988-90 at the peak of world growth but then fell back until 1993. In 1994, as US growth accelerated and Europe and Japan recovered from recession, commodity prices started to pick up again.

US inflation

Commodity prices respond to inflation partly because all prices tend to be dragged up by inflation but also because, for many investors, commodities are one of the best hedges against inflation. The reason that US inflation matters rather than world inflation is only that commodity prices are generally analysed in dollars. Of course inflation is usually a sign that the economy is starting to overheat and that goes along-side strong demand for commodities as inputs, so that it is difficult to separate the two effects.

US interest rates

Again, it is primarily US interest rates that matter when commodity prices are measured in dollars. Low short term interest rates, especially low real interest rates tend to support commodity prices for two reasons. *Firstly*, they make it cheaper to speculate in commodities which of course pay no interest. *Secondly*, low interest rates may be taken as a sign of expansionary monetary policy which, sooner or later, is likely to boost growth and inflation. This was especially the case during the 1970s. Similarly, high interest rates have the opposite effect. Speculation is expensive and high rates may be a prelude to an economic slowdown.

However low interest rates are not necessarily good for commodities if they mean that the economy is very weak and the central bank is having trouble stimulating growth. This helps explain why commodity prices rose in 1994 despite rising interes rates, after being weak in 1992-3 when interest rate were very low.

Categories of Commodities

Commodities can be divided into four broad categories which, to some extent, respond differently to the broad economic influences described above. They are *precious metals* notably gold, *fuels*, especially oil, *industrial raw materials* including metals, timber and cotton and *foods and beverages*, including coffee and tea.

Precious metals

Some investors insist that, to be complete, any portfolio should have a small portion of gold. The reason is that not only is gold an inflation hedge but it also benefits from political uncertainty. Moreover, what makes gold important for some investors, in countries which may not be politically stable in the long run, is that it is portable.

While investors see gold as something that might hold its value in times of inflation or political uncertainty, economists tend to be dismissive of gold because it has very little use-value. There are a few small industrial uses and of course it is used in jewellery but gold's value to investors is simply that everyone agrees that it is the money of last resort.

In the 19th century and into the early years of this century the gold standard was used to peg national currencies, giving gold a central role. Under the Bretton Woods system there was effectively a gold exchange standard which meant that, although not every dollar was necessarily backed by an amount of gold, the US Treasury was committed to provide gold to any dollar holder on demand.

With the breakdown of the Bretton Woods system in the 1970s this guarantee was abandoned. As inflation took off gold soared in relation to dollars, reaching (briefly) a high of over $800 in 1980. Most governments still have substantial reserves of gold though a few have sold some in recent years with the gold price being so lack-lustre.

Some economists cling to the idea that gold will one day be restored to the heart of the monetary n, but this looks highly unlikely. While a gold ard can provide a discipline against inflation it means that the general price level is linked to e supply of gold. In the event of a rise in the upply of gold, as for example occurred in the 16th and 17th centuries following the Spanish and Portuguese development of South America, then the general price level tends to rise. If supply is restricted, as seems to be the case this century, the use of a gold standard might force a general decrease in the price level as output increases. For these reasons a return to a gold standard looks extremely unlikely now.

Gold Price ($/ounce)

Source: DATASTREAM

One factor unique to the precious metals is that the total outstanding of these commodities dwarfs the annual production. This means that the price is much less affected by world economic growth and by partial or temporary supply interruptions due to, for example, strikes. Instead prices are affected primarily by expectations for inflation and interes rates and by political uncertainty.

Fuels

Oil prices have played a central role in the economic history of the last two decades. This reflects a number of factors. One is that, in terms of value, fuels including oil account for around half of all commodities produced. A rise in oil prices therefore has a far more pronounced effect on the industrial countries than a rise in, say, industrial metals prices. Oil can therefore be a very important inflation hedge because it directly impacts the general price level.

Another reason for oil's importance is that a substantial amount of supply comes from the Middle East which has frequently proved unstable. The first oil crisis in 1973 was linked to the Yom Kippur war and the Arab oil embargo while the second, in 1979-80 was linked to the Iran-Iraq war. In 1990 oil prices rose briefly after Iraq's invasion of Kuwait.

Finally of course there has been the role of OPEC, the Organisation of Petroleum Exporting Countries. In practice OPEC's grasp of oil prices has never looked very strong. Briefly in 1973-4 there were restrictions on oil shipments but for most of the period since then OPEC has had difficulty agreeing and sticking to agreed quotas.

For the poorer OPEC members, especially the smaller ones, over-producing could be justified by the need for revenues and the limited impact of a small extra supply on the price. At the same time the rich Gulf countries, several of them relatively large suppliers, notably Saudi Arabia and Kuwait, have had a strong incentive to keep prices moderate for two reasons. *Firstly*, as very low cost producers, they have an incentive not to see prices too high which would choke off demand in the long term. *Secondly*, given the strong economic and security links with the United States, they have an incentive not to disrupt the industrial countries too much.

The worst moment for OPEC came in 1986 when, unable to agree on new quotas, the oil price plunged sharply to only $10 per barrel. This fall came as a surprise to many people because for most of the arly 1980s it had been assumed that oil prices could only go up. Economic forecasters routinely assumed that oil prices would rise by 3-5% p.a. in real terms, i.e. after inflation. In fact since 1986 oil prices, although up somewhat, have remained weak in real terms. Prices have held up in the 1990s with the help of a reduction in Russian production and the limitation on Iraqi exports, under the UN embargo.

Oil Price per barrel

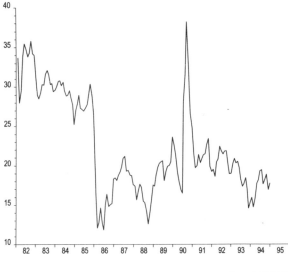

Source: DATASTREAM

Oil remains important but has gradually become much less of a threat to the industrial countries than it was in the 1970s. One reason is that OPEC's share of world output has fallen with the increased use of fields in the North Sea and elsewhere. Another is that dependence on oil supply has been much reduced with the development of alternative energy sources, especially nuclear and gas. Many power stations can now operate on oil or coal depending on price and availability.

Still, some analysts worry that demand could again threaten to outstrip supply before the end of the century, suggesting that oil prices could show an uptrend, even without any political upsets. They cite fast world growth and especially rapid growth of energy use in the Asian newly industrialising countries as reasons. Moreover oil is now often the preferred energy source because of its relative cheapness. On the other hand, Iraq's oil production will rise significantly once exports are allowed again while Russian production, which has fallen in recent years, has the potential to increase very substantially.

Industrial raw materials

This category covers a variety of individual commodities including the metals, copper, iron, zinc, lead etc. and agricultural raw materials such as timber, cotton etc. Each has its own story but economic growth and especially growth of the industrial sector, is the most important demand-side influence. In a strong economic upswing as in 1987-8 or 1994, especially if there are worries over inflation, some of these commodities, especially the metals, are liable to rise as a result of speculative pressures.

Economist Metals Price Index

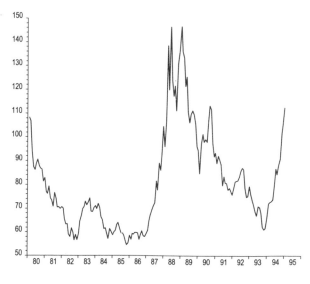

Source: DATASTREAM

Foods and beverages

In this category are both seasonal foods (i.e. they cannot be stored for long) and non-seasonal foods. Prices of the former are very dependent on the weather but, by their nature, there is little scope for speculation except in the very short run. The latter include products such as coffee and orange juice where markets are very active, again often in response to weather or other supply conditions. The most famous supply-side factor is frost in Brazil which periodically devastates the coffee crop. Demand is much less influenced by world growth. Although it will rise with growth it does not show wide swings with the business cycle.

Economist Foods Price Index

Source: DATASTREAM

Long Run Trends in Commodity Prices

The view was prevalent in the 1970s that commodity prices would inevitably be on a long-run up-trend because the world has limited resources and the easy sources of minerals and other commodities would soon be used up, forcing producers to dig deeper or otherwise spend more money on extraction. The experience of rising commodity prices through much of the 1970s seemed to bear out this view.

Before then the prevailing view was that developing countries were in fact doomed to poverty if they persisted in exporting only raw materials because of a tendency for industrial goods prices to rise faster than raw commodity prices. For much of the 20th century this had indeed been the case, the main reason being improved technology in finding and extracting minerals, or in the case of agricultural commodities in growing and harvesting them.

From the perspective of the mid 1990s it looks as though the traditional view was more accurate than the 1970s view. Production costs for most commodities have fallen in real terms and there is little evidence that supplies of commodities are dwindling. New discoveries in new regions or at greater depths continue. Perhaps at some point the world really will start to run out of oil or another key commodity, but there have been fears of this sort for decades or more.

The 1970s experience in fact showed the market in action. A prolonged world upswing in the 1950s and 1960s ended with a rapid boom in the early 1970s, leaving limited capacity in many commodities. But the higher prices of commodities soon produced cutbacks in demand, new sources of supply and alternative products, so that by the 1980s there was widespread over-capacity.

Commodity Indices

There are a range of different commodity indices available but they frequently show different patterns due to different composition and weightings. The Economist commodity indices for example do not include precious metals while the Commodity Research bureau (CRB) index in the US is aimed mainly at commodities traded on US exchanges. One of the best overall indexes is the Goldman Sachs Commodity Index (GSCI) because it weights commodities according to world production.

Commodity Price Indices

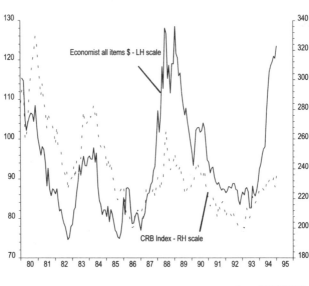

Source: DATASTREAM

Commodities and the investor

For investors then, there is no inevitable up-trend in commodity prices, only cycles. Commodities can be a useful hedge against inflation but are unlikely to be a major part of a portfolio. One effective way to invest is through a fund that invests in the shares of natural resource companies. This provides a stake in commodities themselves but also will do well if the company is successful in reducing costs or finding new resources.

Glossary

The chapters noted at the end of each entry indicate the principal chapter where the term is used.

Arbitrage Pricing Theory (APT). A complex model, part of Modern Portfolio Theory (MPT). *Chapter 8*.

Beta. The key concept in the Capital Asset Pricing Model (CAPM). Beta is a measure of the sensitivity of an individual stock to the market as a whole. For example, if when the market rises (or falls) by 1%, a particular stock rises (or falls) by 2%, then its beta is 2. High beta stocks have higher risk, while stocks with a beta of less than 1 have a lower risk than the market. *Chapter 8*.

Bretton Woods System. The name given to the post-war system of fixed exchange rates which lasted until the early 1970s before breaking down and being replaced with floating rates. It was named after the hotel in the USA where the Allies met in 1944. The IMF and World Bank were also set up following the Bretton Woods conference. *Chapter 9*.

Capacity utilisation. An indicator of the extent to which existing capacity in the form of plant and machinery is in full use. In practice the 100% level is not in itself very meaningful because in Japan the economy is frequently reported as producing at more than 100% of estimated capacity while, for example, in the United States the economy rarely gets above 85%. The US authorities regard 82% as a critical level beyond which inflation will start to rise. *Chapter 3*.

Capital Asset Pricing Model (CAPM). Part of modern portfolio theory (MPT), this model says that the return on a stock can be divided into the return on the market as whole and the specific return from the stock, measured by "beta". *Chapter 8*.

Capital formation. Economists use the word capital in different ways but the underlying concept is the same. The key is that it represents a store of value which is not immediately consumed, i.e., it is either money or a capital good. It cannot be a consumer good which is quickly used up. Capital flight typically means money flowing out of the country. Fixed capital means machinery, factories, etc. while fixed capital formation means investing, i.e. building factories or offices and buying machines to go in them. *Chapter 1*.

Coincident indicators. Data releases which are regarded as normally coincident with the economic cycle. Typical components are industrial production, employment and personal income. This index is not much looked at by the markets (though its individual components are), with much more attention being given to leading indicators. *Chapter 2*.

Comparative advantage. A term much liked by economists and much misunderstood by non economists. A country is said to have a comparative advantage when it can produce one product comparatively more efficiently than another product. This has nothing to do with absolute advantage. For example, India can produce both cotton goods and cars, as can the United States. But in terms of efficiency (or absolute advantage) the United States is more efficient at both if one was simply to count the hours of work that go into producing one or the other, because the United States uses more machines. However, India has a comparative advantage in cotton because of lower wages and availability of cotton at cheap prices. The theory therefore says that India would do well to concentrate upon the good in which it has a comparative advantage rather than trying to produce everything. Then both countries will gain from trade. Note that anybody who says that some countries do not have a comparative advantage in anything are misunderstanding the concept. *Chapter 6*.

Competitiveness. An often mis-used term.
Companies and industries in a particular country
face increasing pressures to be competitive as trade
increases and trade barriers fall. Economists talk of
price competitiveness and non-price
competitiveness, meaning that there is competition
in both price and other factors such as quality and
after sales service. For a country as a whole
competitiveness is assured (at least in the long term)
by changes in exchange rates and/or real wages.
Politicians and others exhorting their countrymen to
become more competitive really should use the word
"productive" or efficient since it is this which will
raise living standards. *Chapter 6*.

Constant prices. Because of the prevalence of
inflation in the last 30 years, economists prefer to
look at many measures of the economy in constant
price terms (as opposed to current prices) to
separate the real from the nominal economy. For
example in current price terms GDP may rise 5% but
after allowing for inflation of 3% the real growth
rate, i.e. in constant price terms is 2%. The difficulty
is that the calculation of prices is not always easy so
that the calculation is much less precise than
statisticians like to pretend. *Chapter 1*.

Consumer confidence. A monthly measure of how
confident consumers feel about the economy, based
on survey data. *Chapter 2*.

Consumption. Economists distinguish consumption
from other forms of spending in order to define it as
goods which are actually consumed, as opposed to
spending which is for investment in the form of
fixed capital or stock building or machinery, etc. In
the national accounts data, consumption also
includes spending on cars and refrigerators, although
technically, since cars last more than one year, the
full spending is not all consumption. In balance
sheet data some allowance is made for this by
including cars and durable goods as a wealth factor.
Chapter 1.

Convertibility. Governments make exchange rates convertible to varying extents. Prior to 1979 for example many countries had what is called current account convertibility. In other words any transactions relating to the current account of the balance of payments, i.e. exports of goods and services or income on investments, was freely convertible by governments. However any investment abroad by a domestic resident or company was subject to some degree of exchange controls. This is the convertibility that countries in Eastern Europe aspire to in order to join the world trading and investment system.

During the 1980s the UK and Japan led many countries including recently many developing countries such as Mexico and Egypt to full convertibility which means that any demand for foreign currency for whatever reason including investment abroad or holding a foreign currency bank account at home is freely available. This trend creates more difficulties for managing currencies but it is believed by the IMF and the World Bank and many others to promote foreign investment in the country and ultimately make for a better economic policy framework and stronger economic growth. *Chapter* 7.

Counter-cyclical. The economy goes through its economic cycle and at times governments want to counter the direction of the cycle. For example in the United States in 1988-89 and again in 1994 the emphasis was on countering the boom and slowing the economy. The main policies that can be used are monetary policy, fiscal policy and exchange rate policy. *Chapter 2*.

Crowding out. The term used to indicate that government borrowing can crowd out other borrowing. Since the availability of credit in the markets is ultimately determined by the level of savings in the economy the existence of too much government borrowing may prevent other borrowing from taking place. Crowding out normally works through interest rates, particularly long term interest rates remaining too high. *Chapter 5*.

Current account. The trade account of countries normally refers to trade in goods only. However US data now includes trade in services as well. Economists generally prefer to look at the current account of the balance of payments (as opposed to the capital account) which includes trade in goods and services plus interest payments and transfers. For most countries trade in services adds between 20-50% to trade in goods although this percentage is on the increase. The current account as measured must then be matched in the balance of payments by the capital account (plus any change in government foreign exchange reserves). As an accounting identity either the current account or the capital account shows the net capital inflow or outflow for the country. *Chapter 6*.

Deflation. This is a term which is used in two different ways. Sometimes it can be used to indicate simply a tightening of policy aimed at slowing the economy but its original meaning meant a decline in the price level. Of course in recent periods a tightening of policy would only slow the rate of inflation, i.e. disinflation, whereas in times past tighter economic policy meant an actual fall in prices. With inflation now only marginally above zero in many countries, most notably Japan, the risk of deflation has become a real one. The particular danger of deflation is that, if people believe that prices will actually fall in the coming months, they will delay spending and that delay in spending can take the economy into a slump and of course take prices down further. This was the pattern in the United States in the early 1930s. *Chapter 3*.

Demand. A popular term among economists to mean spending. An increase in demand therefore could come from consumers or business or government and would be seen and evidenced by a rise in sales. Demand is met by supply, sometimes known as output. *Chapter 1*.

Depression. This is the phase of the business cycle seen only every few decades where either the economy slumps sharply or, as in the so-called Great Depression of the 1870s, it goes through a long period of slow growth and weak profits. Most economists believe that depressions are now much less likely than in the past because of the larger role of government in the economy and tighter official control of the financial system. *Chapter 2*.

Diffusion index. The technical term for the way many leading indicator indices and survey-based composite indices are calculated. The overall index is arrived at by comparing the number of its components that are rising, falling or staying the same. In intuitive terms the idea is that the stronger the economic upswing the more components of the index are likely to be moving up. Approaching a turning point some will turn down before others so this measure should give some warning. *Chapter 2*.

Disinflation. The term used to indicate a policy or process where inflation is brought down. *Chapter 3*.

Disposable income. A technical term used by economists to indicate income after taxation. The difference between what is actually spent on goods and services and disposable income is called savings. Note that the amount spent may include borrowing and indeed during the 1980s saving rates fell mainly because borrowing increased. *Chapter 1*.

Econometrics. This is the branch of economics which produces economic forecasting models and also tests relationships between variables. For example does higher unemployment lead to lower inflation? Essentially this is a mathematical treatment of history and therefore is not always a good guide to the future. Econometrics has become much more sophisticated in recent years, but as has been obvious in the last two-three years, econometric modelling of the economy is still far from a perfect science. In general models seem to be good at forecasting GDP in all the years except where it is important, because it is a turning point of the business cycle! *Chapter 2*.

Effective exchange rate. An index calculated by many central banks of the level of a country's exchange rate in relation to other currencies, on a trade-weighted basis. *Chapter 9*.

Efficient market hypothesis (EMH). The theory that the market price of a stock, or any other asset, already takes into account all the known information and reasonable expectations about the future. *Chapter 8*.

Emerging markets. Term given to the new or newly thriving stock markets of many developing countries. There is no definitive way to distinguish which markets have yet to emerge, which are emerging and which have already emerged. For practical purposes analysts often use the International Finance Corporation (IFC) classifications. The IFC, part of the World Bank, is based in Washington.

Emerging markets are attractive to investors for three reasons. *Firstly*, they often show good long term returns because of the fast underlying growth of GDP and profits. *Secondly*, their returns historically are often non-correlated, i.e. independent of returns in the major markets, so that they provide useful diversification. *Thirdly*, when a market first emerges, or suddenly improves, it can often provide truly spectacular returns. The big downside is that the volatility of emerging markets is much higher than for the developed markets. *Chapter 11*.

Equilibrium. Favourite term of economists, particularly academic economists, to discuss a point to which an economy will tend to move. In practice in the real world, investors will not really see equilibrium and indeed may be trying to take advantage of situations which are far from equilibrium

Exchange controls (see also Convertibility). Exchange controls are attempts by government to control movements of capital either in or out of the capital usually in order to protect an exchange rate. Countries are increasingly removing exchange controls completely (i.e. making the currency fully convertible) because this is seen as a better way to promote investment. *Chapter 6*.

Fiscal policy. The term used by economists to indicate the budgetary stance of the government. *Chapter 5*.

Flow of funds. This is a collection of accounts prepared by government statisticians which show the actual movements of money into different instruments during the course of a year. So, for example, they begin with savings of the household sector and show where those monies are put in terms of investment in house building and purchases of stocks and shares, etc.

Gross Domestic Product (GDP). A statistical calculation of the total flow of goods and services in the economy and as such can be seen as the sum of everybody's income or everybody's spending or everybody's production. Gross domestic product differs from gross national product in that GDP is what is produced in the domestic economy and GNP is what nationals of the country produce, including their income from overseas. *Chapter 1*.

GDP deflator. The inflation index which "deflates" nominal GDP to real GDP. Announced at the same time as real GDP is released, it gives the best overall measure of inflation in the economy. *Chapter 3*.

Gross fixed capital formation. A technical term for investment meaning spending on buildings, plant and machinery, plus spending on constructing residential property. It does not include spending on inventories (though inventories are included in the definition of investment). It is called "gross" because it is calculated without any deduction for depreciation. *Chapter 1*.

High powered money. In countries where banks are required to have a certain percentage of reserve assets in the form of deposits at the central bank, these, together with circulating currency are described as high powered money. Monetary base means the same thing. In principle the central bank can control high powered money and, given the reserve asset ratio, if the authorities allow an increase, then banks can lend out a multiple of this increase. In practice the authorities in most countries do not use this approach because it leads to an extreme volatility in interest rates. The Volcker experiment during 1979 was an attempt to control high powered money and let the interest rate go where it liked but was later abandoned for a far more flexible approach where interest rates are set at a particular level and then altered if the money supply appears to be expanding too fast or too slowly. *Chapter 4*.

Hyper-inflation. A situation of rapidly accelerating inflation. Some countries have inflation of 50-100% p.a. but generally hyper-inflation is the term used for much higher inflation than this. The reason for hyper inflation is also well understood. It can always be traced directly to governments printing money to finance budget deficit. The key to the solution, straightforward in theory, but more difficult in practice, is to close the budget deficit. *Chapter 3*.

Industrial countries. The term applied to the developed countries of Europe, the USA, Canada, Australia, New Zealand and Japan. The usual definition is the OECD group (Organisation for Economic Cooperation and Development based in Paris), though Mexico is now a member and is not usually seen as an industrial country. Other countries, notably Korea, would like to join.

Inventory cycle. A crucial element of the business cycle, also known as the stock cycle. At the beginning of the upswing, businesses decide that sales are likely to grow in future and therefore they start producing for inventory in order to be able to meet that demand when it comes. This extra production can be an important factor in generating the recovery itself. Similarly as recession approaches and business suddenly becomes less confident about future sales, it will try suddenly to reduce inventory by cutting production. However, in so doing, it reduces overtime and earnings and often employment and thereby cuts demand still more. Quite often inventory accumulation or inventory reduction can add or subtract as much as 1-2% growth in the economy in a particular year and thereby is a crucial factor in the economic cycle. *Chapter 2*.

Investment. Economists use the term investment (or capital formation) in a particular way. Investment is defined as spending on something newly produced which will directly provide a good or service later. Hence it includes spending on new buildings, plant and machinery by businesses, etc. which will be used to produce other goods or services later, e.g. factories, offices, machine tools, computers, etc. It also includes spending on inventories, i.e. goods which, for the time being are stored, waiting to be used. It also includes the building of houses, which will provide accommodation in years to come. When an individual or company buys stocks and shares it does not count as investment in economic terms but is described as "accumulation of financial assets". *Chapter 1*.

"J" Curve. This is the path of the trade balance or current account balance in response to devaluation. It traces out the pattern of a "J". At first the trade position gets worse primarily because imports cost more, the downward part of the "J". After a while import volumes fall and exports rise, because of the more competitive exchange rate which makes the trade balance turn around and move up to a level above where it started. *Chapter 6*.

Keynesian. The term used to indicate a view of economics which tends to down play the role of money and monetary policy and emphasise demand (i.e. spending) in the economy and the potential use of fiscal policy. In practice this view of the economy would probably not be recognised by John Maynard Keynes himself, a British economist who died in 1946. Keynes was primarily a monetary economist and his three major economics books all included the word 'money' in the title. Keynesianism, emerging after his death was superficially based on Keynes' hugely influential 1936 book, "The General Theory of Employment Interest and Money". But Keynesian economics got into trouble in the 1970s when it became clear that policy was leading to an increase in inflation and that the supposed trade-off between inflation and unemployment was simply not holding. The ascendancy of the alternative approach, monetarism, however lasted only a few years. Equally there are few economists now who would claim to be unreconstructed Keynesians and who do not put much more emphasis on money than they did twenty years earlier. *Chapter 5*.

Kondratieff cycle. The long cycle of 50 to 60 years first analysed in depth by Kondratieff, a Russian economist writing in the 1920s. *Chapter 2*.

Lags. A term beloved of economists to describe the time interval between one event and another. For example inflation typically peaks some 6 months to a year after the economy peaks and then inflation starts to rise only a year or more into economic recovery. *Chapter 2*.

Leading indicators. Data releases which usually lead (predate) turning points in the economy. By taking a group of indicators the fluctuations in any one indicator are washed out. Typical indicators are average weekly hours, manufacturers' new orders, stock prices, money supply and consumer confidence. Note however that the lead time between the leading indicators indcx and the economy varies considerably and can be as short as 1-2 months. Governments also compile indices of coincident indicators and lagging indicators. *Chapter 2*.

Liquidity trap. This was a term invented by Keynes to indicate a situation where, despite interest rates being very low, nobody wants to borrow to get the economy moving. He identified it in the context of the 1930s when the price level was actually falling and therefore, although interest rates were down at 1%, real interest rates were at 3-4% or more, reflecting the declining price level or deflation of the time. *Chapter 4*.

Macro-economics. Economists divide into macro-economists and micro-economists. The macro-economy is how the overall economy operates and deals with inflation, unemployment, GDP growth, etc., the main subject matter of this book. Micro-economics is concerned with such questions as how companies operate and how to deal with public monopolies.

Monetarism. The view that money growth is closely linked to inflation. The key proponents of monetarism were Irving Fisher who evolved the quantity theory of money and Milton Friedman who promoted monetarism throughout the 1960s and 1970s and who wrote, with Anna Schwarz, "The Monetary History of the United States". *Chapter 4*.

Money illusion. This was the term used particularly in the 1970s to indicate people's unawareness of inflation. By focusing on nominal values people often seemed not to be aware that the real levels were not what they seemed. *Chapter 3*.

NAPM or National Association of Purchasing Managers' reports. A closely watched US monthly data release based on a survey of purchasing managers. A value above 40 indicates that the economy is expanding while a value above 50 indicates that the manufacturing sector is expanding. *Chapter 2*.

Output gap. A gap which opens out in times of recession between the trend growth path of the economy (as calculated) and the actual path. While the output gap is open inflation tends to decline. Once it closes and especially if the economy starts to overheat and go above its trend path, sometimes called an inflationary gap, inflation tends to rise. *Chapter 3*.

Overheating. When the economy grows fast and in particular when it approaches full capacity it is said to exhibit signs of overheating, notably rising inflation, shortages of skilled labour and increasing wages. Also there may be sharp rises in asset prices and in commodity prices. Signs of overheating usually receive a sharp response from the monetary authorities who raise interest rates to slow the economy down. *Chapter 2*.

Phillips curve. A simple scatter chart measuring unemployment on one axis against inflation on the other. Prior to the 1970s at least it seemed to show that high unemployment goes with low inflation and vice-versa. *Chapter 3*.

Price-earnings ratio. The ratio of a stock price to company earnings per share. Usually the PE ratio will use historical earnings, i.e. actual earnings in the latest year, but sometimes it will be quoted using prospective earnings, i.e. analysts' forecasts for the coming year. *Chapter 11*.

Productivity. Defined as output per unit of input employed. The most useful measure is labour productivity, i.e. the amount of output per man-hour. It can be measured as, for example, the number of cars produced per worker in a year. More commonly it will be measured as the value of output per man hour. Provided that a good measure of inflation is used over time, then changes in productivity can be measured. Clearly the income levels of a country depend crucially on labour productivity. Poor countries have relatively low productivity while the rich countries have high levels. Ultimately what determines productivity is the amount of machinery available to support labour, the effectiveness of the organisation of production (i.e. how efficient is it) and the skills of the workforce. *Chapter 1*.

Recession. A period of declining GDP. In the United States the National Bureau of Economic Research defines recession as 2 consecutive quarters of declining GDP. Other countries do not use such a precise definition. Sometimes the term growth recession is used to describe a period of slower growth than normal. Recessions are distinguished from depressions by the extent of the downturn. A depression is associated with the experience of the 1930s when output slumped by 10% or more in most countries. *Chapter 2*.

Recovery. The term used for the end of a recession. The US National Bureau of Economic Research defines the trough as the lowest month in the recession, i.e. just before output turns around and begins to rise again. The recovery therefore starts the month after the trough. It ends when the economy regains the same level of output it had immediately prior to the recession. This normally takes a year or more of increased output. *Chapter 2*.

Savings. Defined by economists as the difference between current income and current spending. Note that it could be negative if people borrow. *Chapter 1*.

Supply-side. The supply-side of the economy comprises the decisions to produce, how much and at what price. The emergence of supply-side economics in the 1980s was a reminder that the key determinant of incomes, especially in the longer run, is the efficient use and allocation of labour and capital in the economy. Supply-siders emphasized the importance of low taxation and reduced regulation to encourage increased productivity and output. This can be contrasted with demand-side economics which focuses on spending decisions. Both Keynesian economics and monetarism are primarily focused on the demand-side. *Chapter 1.*

Trade cycle. An alternative word for business cycle. *Chapter 2.*

Trend growth rate. A concept beloved of economists which aims to show the average growth rate that the economy can attain for a long period, 5-10 years or more, even though the actual economy may cycle around this trend. The components of the trend growth rate can be broken down into labour force growth rate and the rate of growth of labour productivity. Also sometimes called potential growth rate or underlying growth rate. *Chapter 1.*

Underlying growth rate. See Trend growth rate. *Chapter 1.*

Unit labour costs. Wage costs per unit of output. In effect, if wages are rising by 4% and productivity growth by 3% then unit labour costs rise by 1%. *Chapter 1.*

Velocity of money. The speed at which money flows around the economy. *Chapter 4.*

Volatility. Describes the size of fluctuations in the market price of a security. High volatility is associated with high risk. A crucial part of option pricing. *Chapter 8.*

Yield curve. The range of interest rates from overnight rates to 30 year bonds or more. *Chapter 4.*

PROBUS PUBLISHING COMPANY

Probus Publishing Company is a major force on the international business and finance publishing scene. We are committed to publishing the very finest books and information products. Our range of quality books in core business subjects such as investments, banking, the capital markets, accountancy, taxation, property, insurance, sales management, marketing and healthcare, is second to none. We believe that you will find many other titles in our range to be of interest. Are you a writer? If so please feel free to refer potential publications to us.

You may wish to contact Probus Publishing Company direct at:

1333 Burr Ridge Parkway OR	11 Millers Yard
Burr Ridge	Mill Lane
IL 60521	Cambridge CB2 1RQ
USA	England
Tel: (708) 789-4000	Tel: (01223) 322018
Tel [Sales]: 800-631-3966 [USA only]	Fax: (01223) 61149
Fax: (708) 789-6933	

The Global Investor: Opportunities, Risks and Realities for Institutional Investors in the World's Markets
Gavin R Dobson
300 pages, Probus Publishing Company, 1994.
ISBN 1 55738 556 4

Gavin Dobson is CEO of one of the fastest growing investment funds in the world, specializing in emerging markets and EAFE emerging market equity management. In this book, he reveals the secrets of the world's top fund managers, based upon his own *practical* experience of looking after over $500 million. By the time you read this, it may be a billion.

Maybe you aspire to being worth millions, or would like to be an investment manager. Maybe you would just like to know how the world of investment works. Whatever the case, this book will give you the answers. Written in a clear accessible way, it will give the reader an overview of the history of investment, along with an understanding of strategies, practices, administration and how to interpret global trends for your own benefit. Buy this book **now** before you make another investment move.

The Capital Markets Diary 1996
240 pages, Probus Publishing Company, 1995.
ISBN 1 55738 926 8

Ever wondered why no one seems to be able to come up with a diary that really suits your needs as a finance professional? So did we. That is why we created *The Capital Markets Diary*. After consulting traders, investment managers, analysts, economists, consultants and others, we have made sure that this desk diary clearly presents *what you really want and need* - in the right format.

The special features include:

■ **Section I - Information**
● Year Planner 1996 ● Calendars 1996-98
● Underground and Metro Maps ● City Centre Maps
● International Direct Dialling and World Times
● Capital Markets Associations ● Central and National Banks ● Securities Regulators ● Financial Exchanges Worldwide ● National Statistical Offices ● News Agencies ● Glossary of Financial Terms in 5 Languages (English, French, German, Italian and Spanish)

■ **Section II - Business Travel and Services**
● Travel/Entertainment/Sport/Services for the Key Financial Centres: Amsterdam, Brussels, Copenhagen, Frankfurt, Hong Kong, London, Madrid, New York, Paris, Singapore, Stockholm, Sydney, Tokyo, Washington DC, Zurich ● World Airlines

■ **Section III - 1996 Diary and Features**

■ **Section IV - Personal Forms**
● Expenses ● Car Expenses ● Staff Holidays
● Personal Investment Records

Beautifully produced and designed, the diary is 240 pages in length, A4 page size, hardback, with discreet 'wiro' binding to ensure that the pages lie flat in use.

As a valued customer, please accept our offer of a specially reduced price of £29.95 (normal price £45.00).

To reserve copies, just contact either of the addresses given at the beginning of the section.

The 'ALL ABOUT' series

Each book in this popular series has been written by an expert in the field. Together, they cover almost every aspect of modern finance and investment. Their contents work perfectly well as an introduction for beginners or alternatively as a refresher course for veterans.

Titles include:

All About Stocks: From the Inside Out. *Esme Faerber*
225 pages, Probus Publishing Company, 1995.
ISBN 1 55738 806 7

All About Bonds: From the Inside Out. *Esme Faerber*
250 pages, Probus Publishing Company, 1993.
ISBN 1 55738 437 1

All About Options: From the Inside Out.
Russell Wasendorf & Thomas McCafferty
250 pages, Probus Publishing Company, 1993.
ISBN 1 55738 434 7

All About Futures: From the Inside Out.
Russell Wasendorf & Thomas McCafferty
250 pages, Probus Publishing Company, 1992.
ISBN 1 55738 296 4

All About Commodities: From the Inside Out.
Russell Wasendorf & Thomas McCafferty
250 Pages, Probus Publishing Company, 1992.
ISBN 1 55738 459 2

All About Mutual Funds: From the Inside Out. *Bruce Jacobs*
250 pages, Probus Publishing Company, 1994.
ISBN 1 55738 807 5

All About Real Estate Investing: From the Inside Out.
William Benke & Joseph M Fowler
200 pages, Probus Publishing Company, 1995.
ISBN 1 55738 882 2

The Vest Pocket Investor - Everything You Need to Know to Invest Successfully
Jae K. Shim, Joel G. Siegel

300 pages, Probus Publishing Company, 1995.
ISBN 1 55738 813 X

The one book every investor needs. Written by the authors of the top-selling *The Vest Pocket MBA, The Vest Pocket Investor* is an authoritative, easy-to-understand overview of every aspect of investment. In clear, straightforward language, the authors describe the instruments, the strategies and the principles of successful investing. Covering everything from funds to options to sources of investment information, this book provides an answer to virtually every investment question that may arise. For beginning and experienced investors alike, *The Vest Pocket Investor* will prove to be a lifelong source of investment wisdom. Specific topics include:

- Advantages and disadvantages of stocks, bonds, funds, annuities, futures & options
- Understanding risk and return
- How to choose a specific stock, bond or fund
- Building an investment portfolio
- Sources of investment information

Wall Street Words - From Annuities to Zero Coupon Bonds (Revised Edition) *Richard J. Maturi*
175 pages, Probus Publishing Company, 1995.
ISBN 1 55738 865 2

Richard Maturi provides a concise explanation of the investment markets, and defines and explains hundreds of words and terms. A perfect book for the average investor, the revised edition of *Wall Street Words* is completely updated and includes dozens of new entries. Most importantly, the book discusses the potential risks and rewards associated with various investment strategies and demonstrates how investors can determine whether a particular strategy is appropriate for them. Authoritative and easy to understand, *Wall Street Words* is a book that investors will use over and over again. Specific features include:

- Dividend reinvestment strategies
- Convertible bonds and stocks
- Penny stocks
- Understanding options

**The Dictionary of Banking: Over 4,000 Terms
Defined and Explained**
Charles J Woelfel
225 pages, Probus Publishing Company, 1995.
ISBN 1 55738 728 1

Put this book on your shelf to guarantee that you are
never baffled by banking jargon again! It acts as a training
resource, memory refresher and experienced guide
through the complexities of global banking. Command of
the language used in modern banking is half the battle
and this book is a powerful tool in helping you to win.

Developed and compiled by the author of the industry-
standard *Encyclopedia of Banking & Finance, The
Dictionary of Banking* is a valuable asset for you, your
bank and your colleagues. This unique and independent
reference guide is user-friendly, accessible, portable and
affordable. You will return to this book again and again -
bank on it.

The Encyclopedia of Banking & Finance
Charles J Woelfel
1200 pages, Probus Publishing Company, 1994.
ISBN 1 55738 396 0 (10th Edition)

This is the finance industry's best-selling reference
classic. Bankers have turned to *The Encyclopedia of
Banking & Finance* for over 70 years because this handy,
authoritative volume answers almost any question about
finance that could arise. From 'Abandonment of Title' to
'Zero-Coupon Bonds', it is all here.

In addition to defining thousands of banking, business
and financial tools, *The Encyclopedia* includes a wide
array of useful statistical, analytical and historical tools,
such as: mathematical formulac and financial
performance ratios; historical data on everything from
money supply to the prime rate; industry information
affecting investment and lending evaluations; legal and
regulatory references; and an international banking
perspective.

Dictionary of Futures & Options: Over 1,500 International Terms Defined and Explained
Alan Webber
240 pages, Probus Publishing Company, 1994.
ISBN 1 55738 595 5

The Dictionary of Futures & Options is a comprehensive source of essential information for anyone involved in the futures and options markets throughout the world. As well as all the basic terminology, there are substantial descriptions of options strategies, the 'Greek' letters, position exposure to certain measures and more. It is an excellent training aid, professional tool and general reference guide.

If you deal with derivatives, gear yourself up with this book and keep on top of one of the hottest areas in finance. Remember, you could be in trouble if you lose your bearings without this excellent reference...

An Introduction to Commodities Futures & Options (Second Edition) *Nick Battley*
160 pages, Probus Publishing Company, 1995.
ISBN 1-55738-920-9

"*An Introduction to Commodity Futures & Options* is one of the most helpful introductions to commodity derivatives I have come across."
-Trevor Christmas, Director of Business Development, International Petroleum Exchange

This second edition of a very popular work provides a straightforward yet authoritative introduction which assumes no prior knowledge of the subject. It gives the reader a wealth of invaluable practical information that includes:

● a clear, concise explanation of market theories and operations

● their practical applications

● risk management strategies for purchasing and supply

● valuable insights into the problem of malpractice (including discussion of the Nick Leeson/Barings debacle)

● full use and definition of in 'in-house' terminology

● listing of major exchanges and their contracts

● a unique illustrated guide to over 50 of the hand signals used in pit trading

The World's Futures & Options Markets
Nick Battley
1029 pages, Probus Publishing Company, 1994.
ISBN 1 55738 513 0

The essential reference work for everyone with a
professional or personal interest in futures and options.
This major publication features detailed information on:
over 550 contracts, categorized by type and listed
alphabetically for ease of reference; the World's 51
derivatives exchanges; and country overviews.

Packed with vital details for most forms of analysis and
presented in an easily accessible way, this book should be
on the shelf of anyone serious about futures & options.
The editor combined his years of *practical* experience in
the markets, with the latest information from individuals,
companies and exchanges to create the most accessible,
useful guide to the world's derivatives markets currently
available.

The Reuters Guide to Official Interest Rates (Second Edition) *Ken Ferris & Mark Jones*
224 pages, Probus Publishing Company, 1995.
ISBN 1 55738 925 X

Who is responsible for changing official interest rates?
What are the domestic and international considerations?
What are the key rates to watch? How do central banks
control the money market? What is the link between
official interest rates and commercial rates charged by
banks? *The Reuters Guide* answers all these questions and
is the only book available that deals exclusively with
official interest rates and how central banks change
monetary policy. The vital rate information about the
twenty largest market economies in the book includes:

● Who controls the interest rate levels

● How the official interest rates are linked

● How central banks control their money markets

● How to use your Reuters terminal to pick out the vital
  facts

In addition, there the book has a 'tear out and keep'
personal organiser card that lists all the key Reuters
codes.